THE
KINGDOM
OF
INDIVIDUALS

THE KINGDOM OF INDIVIDUALS

An Essay on Self-Respect and Social Obligation

F. G. Bailey

CORNELL UNIVERSITY PRESS

Ithaca and London

First published 1993 by Cornell University Press.

International Standard Book Number 0-8014-2811-4 (cloth)
International Standard Book Number 0-8014-8078-7 (paper)
Library of Congress Catalog Card Number 92-29723

Printed in the United States of America

Librarians: Library of Congress cataloging information appears on the last page of the book.

⊗ The paper in this book meets the minimum requirements of the American National Standard for Information Sciences–Permanence of Paper for Printed Library Materials, ANSI Z39.48-1984.

Contents

Preface

This book, I realize now that it is written, is about a lifetime's discomfort with hierarchy and authority, with the experience of being instructed what to do and, directly or indirectly, discouraged from asking why. If, as a child, you miss the message and do ask why, you will likely be invited to collude in your own submission, being told "Because it is right!" That is very different from a threat of punishment or the promise of a reward; threats and promises are straightforward, because they give you the chance to think the matter through and decide what is in your interest. But when you are told to do something because it is right, your *interests* are not involved: your *conscience* is. You are not invited to think the matter through for yourself: quite the reverse. You are told to have faith; be a true-believer. What conscience, oddly enough, has in common with authority is that both tell you to let someone else or something else do your thinking for you and make your decisions.

On the other hand it is sometimes a relief to be told what to do. Besides, who would want to live in a world—almost un-imaginable—where everyone constantly played the child's re-gressive game of always asking why? Nothing would ever be done.

The issue is a perennial in the gardens of philosophy. Recall how Rousseau opened *The Social Contract*: "Man is born free; and everywhere he is in chains. One thinks himself the master of others, and still remains a greater slave than they." It is, he adds, an arrangement that is "legitimate"; it is good that people are everywhere in chains. Rousseau is playing a game with his readers. The chains, it turns out, have nothing to do with force, jails, or prison cells. They are *conventions*, the basic agreements on which society depends for its orderliness; with-out those "chains" we would all end up in an abyss of social chaos.

The same metaphor appears at the end of *The Communist Manifesto*. "The proletarians have nothing to lose but their chains." This time there is no game; chains connote imprison-ment, force, loss of liberty, loss of identity, deprivation, and exploitation; they are not legitimate.

Life is difficult—or perhaps challenging—because we con-stantly experience chains in both those senses. We know that our continued existence depends upon social groups and the conventions they impose on individual behavior. Workers in factories, soldiers in armies, students in schools and colleges, women in households, ordinary citizens hemmed in by the bu-reaucracy—none of them would survive without the protecting framework of society and its institutions. At the same time all to some degree resent what they are being made to do; but, unlike Marx's hoped-for revolutionaries, most of them most of the time do not see salvation in taking power themselves and abolishing the institutions that make life unpleasant for them, because they believe they are dependent on those institutions, and sometimes they cannot conceive of life without them. All they seek is a limit to the power that others exercise over them, and perhaps, sometimes, a chance to make the bosses pay for something they are not getting.

The issue and its congeners are indeed perennials. Still into the twentieth century they occupy a prominent place in social philosophy. How does one make the connection between the micro-level and the macro-level of social analysis? How does one link agency with structure, action with institutions? What does near-focus ethnography contribute to our understanding of change in larger social formations? How closely do those larger formations constrain the detailed behavior that ethnography reveals? Does ethnographic description confront structural theory with reality and so test it? These are some of the ways in which the problem of the individual and the collectivity manifests itself.

This book is mostly an ethnography, a personal and selective recollection of my own experiences, and an indirect statement of my attitudes. When I give meaning to the experiences, making use of one or another kind of social theory, it is more in the spirit of "So that is what it was all about!" than with a desire to sell this theory of agency or that theory of institutions. The experience rules, and whatever theory makes sense of it is put to use.

Nevertheless some issues in the agency-structure debate were settled (for me) a long time ago.[1] Much of the literature is rhetoric that elevates one framework and downplays the other. But in practice (as well as in logic) the paired concepts require each other. A theory of institutions leaves much unexplained if it is not matched with a theory of agency; and vice versa. Without attention to agency there is no way to explain how social formations ever change as conditions external to them change; without the concept of structure or institution there is no way of describing what is changing.

[1] See Bailey 1960.

A matter which has more recently become clear to me is the connection between power and conscience—*conscience* in the sense of knowing what is the right thing to do. As an individual I am controlled in two ways: from inside by my conscience, that is, by conventions (and the institutions which those conventions serve to maintain) and from outside by people who exercise power over me. It is somewhat paradoxical that the first kind—internalized values—can provoke resentment (which often is blurred by a feeling of guilt).[2] More common, I suspect, and certainly part of my own experience, is the unqualified resentment that arises when I see my internalized values misappropriated by others who use them to manipulate me. That is the feeling I described in the opening sentences of this preface. In other words, those who direct institutions, those who have authority, in practice often own the institutions and exploit them for their own benefit. Rousseau's chains turn out, after all, to be just like the Marxist chains, instruments of domination. When I perceive this is happening, I withhold my consent, refusing legitimacy to the rulers: if they want me to obey them, they must either pay me or intimidate me. Of course, if I am unaware of what is being done, I follow my conscience and collude unknowingly in my own subjection.

I also have a bias that is certainly not rational. I do not like true-believers in either direction, but especially I mistrust those philosophies that push the pendulum far to the right, resolutely sublating individuals and empowering only collectivities. It is not simply that they leave questions unanswered. That is to be expected; every theory does the same. What I find distressing is that the proponents of those philosophies build themselves the intellectual equivalent of a convent, an ivory tower, an exclusive club of true-believers whose sense of superiority over nonbelievers is quite effortless and never re-

---

[2] I discuss this in Chapter 6 with reference to family life.

flexively questioned; ideas are transformed into scriptures. Even that would be tolerable, if they really did live in an ivory tower; but they do not. They use their scriptures to work on the world around them, and periodically they propel it into disaster. No less unfortunate is a rampant hypocrisy which denies that this philosophy has anything to do with domination.[3] But I will try to be objective, since I also know that those who push the pendulum too far the other way, toward agency, are equally tunnel-visioned. Besides, if they had their way, they would certainly create a life that would be, in the melodic words of Thomas Hobbes, solitary, poor, nasty, brutish, and short.

Three questions about the balance between individualism and its opposite will concern me: First, what can people do to push the process in one direction or the other? Second, what (in more detail than is given here) are the consequences of moving the pendulum left or right? Third, what are the contexts that allow one or the other philosophy to dominate?

The story, told in three parts, is about a never-ending contest between the scientific attitude and religion, between questioning and true-belief, between the critics and the faithful. The first part (Chapter 1) contests the pervasive spirit of collectivism that has marked the social sciences (other than economics), and insists that individualism is a reality manifested in *disengagement*—what individuals do to prevent themselves from being entirely incorporated into collectivities. The second part is about tactics: about what organizations do to give themselves legitimacy and make obedience a matter of conscience (Chapter 2); about the forms of *symbolic* reassertion that individuals use to preserve their identity (Chapter 3); and about the *practical* measures available for individuals to escape instrumental coercion by organizations (Chapter 4). The final part looks into situations that bolster one or the other sentiment. Chapter 5,

[3]This argument is made in Bailey 1991a.

after describing experiences that elevate the sense of being an individual, argues that organizations defeat themselves if they succeed in regimenting individualism out of existence. The final chapter, on the family and on experiences in the Second World War, demonstrates that ambiences maximally marked by the spirit of collectivism yet contain the source of their own inversion.

Books, especially academic books, are often written about other books, not about any direct experience that the writer has had of the world. The world of experience comes into the picture in the end, but at several removes: the critic insists on the beauty or fatuity of A's ideas about B's ideas about C's ideas about what goes on in the world. Of course the ideas have to be there; one cannot convey an experience without giving it meaning, and that is what ideas do. The simple notion of what anthropologists do (simple before the "writing culture" people[4] threw their hats in the ring) was that anthropologists convey through their writing the ideas that some particular set of people have about their world and how it works and should work—A's (the anthropologist's) ideas about B's (the native's) ideas about B's world. This subject-viewing-object formulation, the writing culture scholars have made clear, conceals the unhappy fact that in their writing anthropologists (A, the subject) are likely to misrepresent, distort, exploit, and in various ways do violence to the integrity of the native (B, the object).

This book is different, in that much of it is about my own experiences; I am both A and B. To that extent I am my own Other, dialogic within myself (as should be clear from what is ambivalently written above and below about structure and agency). I am being authentically represented, in a rather literal way. The question *Who speaks for whom?* should not arise. But perhaps it does. First, the "I" who now writes is no longer

[4]To make a beginning see Clifford and Marcus 1986.

the "I" who experienced; therefore it is quite possible that I am exploiting me, a novel kind of reflexivity. Second, I have an obvious incentive to paint out the warts; I am not aware of having done so. Of course I have prejudices; I have tried to make clear in this Preface what they are, and, as the narrative proceeds, the reader can probably work out where they originate. Third, I do speak for others every time I put myself into a category (schoolboy, soldier, student, and so forth); but I still speak as a native more than is usually the case in an ethnography. Fourth, obviously, the dialogue is not within myself alone; it is a confrontation between my ideas and what others have written that accords neither with my experience of the world nor with my values.

For their comments and suggestions I am grateful to Roy D'Andrade, Paula Levin, Michael Meeker, and Mary K. Olsen. I also thank James S. Coleman and T. N. Madan, editors respectively of *Rationality and Society* and of *Contributions to Indian Sociology*, for comment on arguments advanced here that also appear in those journals.

F. G. BAILEY

Del Mar, California

THE
KINGDOM
OF
INDIVIDUALS

Chapter 1

Disengaging within Collectivities

Under the crust of bureaucracy, quiet behind the posters,
Unconscious but palpably there—the Kingdom of
    individuals.
                    —Louis MacNeice, "The Kingdom"

BREAKING THE CRUST

Having spent much of my life within the framework of
formally organized collectivities (a school, an army in wartime,
and several universities, not to mention nine cities, a village in
India and another in Italy and another in Britain, and four
countries), I know that there is often friction between collectivities and the individuals who are part of them, because the
individuals consider that the collectivity is giving too little and
asking too much. The friction may be chronic, like arthritis, or
it may be episodic, like an outbreak of flu. Metaphors of illness
are often used by those in authority, for it is part of their creed
to deplore apathy or disgruntlement in the servants of an organization. Also, of course, authorities do not relish the disrespect for themselves implied in such attitudes. I have noticed,
however, that from the other direction—from outside or from

below—such conflicts, so far from being always seen as an affliction, sometimes serve as a tonic and are observed, or even entered into, with barely concealed relish, or sometimes, if there is no danger, with unconcealed enjoyment. Disrespect, it seems, can be invigorating.

Organizations are made uncomfortable by uncertainty. What is not predictable cannot be controlled by advance planning, must be negotiated when it surfaces, and consequently makes a mockery of large-scale operations, which are the hallmark of bureaucracies, because every new occasion is a new negotiation. The difference is analogous to buying flour, already packaged and labeled, in a fixed-price store and buying it in a bazaar in India, where each transaction is a unique and adversarial encounter between buyer and seller, a haggle over price and quality, because the buyer cannot predict with certainty the quality of what is being bought or even, sometimes, the quantity; sellers have many ways of cheating. The only strategy for the buyer, if not to patronize fixed-price stores, is to develop a personal relationship of mutual trust with the marketperson.

Buying service from people always has in it an element of a bazaar transaction. Since people are not standardized and one never knows exactly what one is buying, the organization's best strategy is to standardize its servants, to homogenize them, at least with respect to making their loyalty to the organization predictably secure. In both cases—the bazaar and the organization—expediency ("What am I getting out of this?") is replaced or at least tempered by ethical considerations ("What *should* I be putting into this?"). In the case of the formal organization, the pattern of ethics that is imposed, emphasizing duty, puts the organization in a privileged position. The employees are no longer employees; they have become an integral part of the organization, morally involved, and what is good for it is by definition good for them. There is no question about where priority lies: it lies with the collectivity. The whole is greater than the sum of its parts and therefore (at least in this rhetoric) certainly greater than any one of them: that doctrine is called *holism*. Its contrary is *individualism*.

THE INDIVIDUAL

The notion of an individual and of individual freedom is elusive for sure, and sometimes seems illusory. We are accustomed, in everyday speech, to make an easy opposition between individual and society. But, as is well known, there are problems in separating individuals, as independent and autonomous entities, from collectivities.[1]

At first sight it is not so difficult. Stones (individuals) make up a wall (society), and the stones have features that existed before the wall was built, and the wall also has characteristics that are not reducible to the features of the stones built into it. (The wall also has properties that *do* depend on the properties of the stones. A granite wall is not like a sandstone wall with respect to weathering.) The individual—the stone on its own—also has features, we assume, that give him or her a distinct identity. But what are those features? The problem is that it is hard to think of us having an independent prior existence, as the stones did before they went into the wall. "I think: therefore I am," said Descartes. But how I think does not come entirely from me; it comes also from the society in which I live. Everyone is born into a tradition that provides directions not only about how to behave but also how to think and find meaning in what happens. Again, it is commonly said that the individuals should be free to fulfill themselves and realize their

[1]Quick access to this debate can be gained by reading Phillips 1976 or Lukes 1973. Also useful, if somewhat more exacting, is Giddens 1979.

potentialities, unhampered by the collectivity. But is not fulfillment itself socially defined, and how could it be achieved
outside the framework of a society?

I am a body and a nervous system and an inheritance of
genes, a biological organism. But I am also more than a body.
Our problems—organizations and their recalcitrant members—are social, not biological. Of course my biological inheritance will surely influence my social performance; but that is
not the issue. The issue is morality. For genetic reasons I may
do things that my society considers immoral, but it is not ge-
netics that defines morality. We are more than biological organisms; we are organisms equipped also with moral sensi-
tivity. The individual is, to quote a French scholar whose
thoughts will provide a convenient foil for my discussion, "the
independent, autonomous, and thus (essentially) non-social
moral being, as found primarily in our modern ideology of man
and society" (Dumont 1977:8; emphasis in original). In that
phrase "non-social *moral* being" Dumont is pointing up what
he sees as a contradiction: the idea that one can be both nonsocial and moral. Whether or not he is correct in that opinion,
and whether or not *individual* in practice must mean a wholly
nonsocial entity, are central issues in this book.[2]

The debate about the position of the individual in society
goes on at two levels. One level is about ethics and it is a
question of rights and duties: Which takes precedence, individuals and their rights or the collectivity to which they owe duties? The other level is epistemological or methodological and
concerns the framework to be used to understand the relationship between individual and society. Which *logically* comes first
in a theory of society: the individual or the society? These two
approaches in principle are independent. An analytical framework is not simultaneously and necessarily a moral imperative.

---

[2]A more detailed discussion of Dumont's ideas on holism is to be found
in Bailey 1991a.

But the matter is not so simple, and the answer to the analytical question can be used, rhetorically, to support whatever answer one gives to the moral question; or moral conviction can shape the analysis. To make this clear I will briefly summarize the debate about man in society, first outlining the case for individualism.

The argument begins by asserting that it is uncommon, to say the least, for people in any culture at any time voluntarily to inflict pain upon themselves. When they do deliberately damage their bodies, the incident is domesticated by saying either that the occasion is abnormal (firewalking or chopping off a finger joint to stimulate a vision) or that the people themselves are sick. Normal people, it is asserted, are programed to look after themselves; they do so instinctively and cannot avoid doing so. That is human nature: it is found in all cultures. More than that, experience seems to show that people, left to themselves, will look to their own gratification, even when they know that their actions harm other people. The tendency to trample on others has to be restrained because unrestrained conflict, which characterizes unregulated social interaction, would cause chaos and so prevent individual needs from being satisfied.

The assertion that people look to themselves first, even at the cost of others' well-being, itself rests on an indisputable assumption that the biological individual has psychophysical needs—for food, for shelter, for sex, perhaps for companionship—and if those needs were not satisfied, human life would not continue. Therefore, it is argued, society exists. Its function is to impose moral standards in order to provide for individuals and their needs. Therefore it is appropriate to explain the characteristics of a society from the assumed needs and characteristics of its individuals. Therefore also it is appropriate to judge social forms as good or bad, according to how well they serve individual needs.

The counterargument runs like this. Of course biological individuals have psychophysical needs. But the individual in society is by definition a social or moral individual, not simply a biological organism. If we wish to understand a pattern of social interaction, then we must pay attention to the individual more as a moral being and less as a biological organism. A focus on morality entails a focus on society, for it is there that the moral order is located. This is inescapably true of all societies at all times. Furthermore, those arguments that start from the premise of an autonomous presocial individual—"man in a state of nature"—rest on nothing more than a poetic vision, a mythical reconstruction of a state of affairs that never existed except in fantasy. The men and women who are in reality experienced by us in our everyday life are the products of a social environment and are born into a social world that provides them with ideas and values; they are not merely biological organisms but also moral beings. Society shapes the moral individual and therefore, logically, comes first. Furthermore, to know a person is nothing other than to know that person's pattern of relationships. When we have understood the principles on which a society is constructed, we have all that we need in order to understand, from a sociological point of view, the conduct of social persons. To postulate an individual as an entity that exists apart from the social person is an epistemological and, indeed, metaphysical error.[3] Moreover, to put the origin of society in the individual's needs is not only to invite a failure in understanding but also (by thus giving legitimacy to self-interested actions) to further the breakdown of the social order.

Both these doctrines, as epistemological constructs, are easily carried over into the moral domain; and I have done so in the concluding sentence of each of the three preceding paragraphs. The individual who has logical priority is also the one

---

[3]The argument itself is obviously in error, since it equates "individual" with "social person," thus asserting, indisputably but not usefully, that all white swans are white.

who has inalienable rights against society. Social institutions are to be evaluated by the efficiency with which they serve individual interests. From the other point of view the individual is less the possessor of rights than the bearer of duties, serving the collectivity. The political implications of these two philosophies are a recurring theme in this book.

SVEJKISM

Philosophizing apart, there is a plausible everyday explanation as to why organized collectivities should be privileged at the expense of individuals. Inasmuch as we all live in societies and therefore depend upon other people for our continued existence, the golden rule that we should do unto others as we would have them do unto us seems incontrovertible. From that point it is not difficult to take a further step and conclude that the collectivity (which, of course, consists of other people, who are by definition in the majority) is always right and must always have priority over the interests of individuals (in the minority, also by definition), if the latter interests happen not to coincide with those of the collectivity. "The board must, at all times, act in what is the best interest of the membership of the entire community. The individual interests of a particular homeowner must be overridden by the board's concern for the community as a whole."[4]

Moreover, to continue this cavalier line of reasoning, since at the present day the larger collectivities that we most directly experience come to us in the form of bureaucracies—the city manifests itself to us powerfully as city hall—the bureaucracies

[4]Letter to the *Los Angeles Times*, July 13, 1991. The occasion, somewhat comic, was a public reprimand for lewd conduct in the parking lot ("kissing and doing bad things"), delivered by a condominium board to one of the residents, a grandmother. It turned out to be a case of mistaken identity.

themselves appear to be a kind of public good, something to which selfish narrow interests must be subordinated in the interests of us all. The organization can then claim to be no more than altruism translated into action.

That claim does not go unchallenged. I am thinking not of explicit challenges, revolution or rebellion or constitutional challenge through the courts or through elections, but rather of disengagement,[5] a convenient term for an unobtrusive or indirect way in which individuals protect themselves from organizational or institutional exploitation.[6] In some bureaucracies one can find fully matured forms of disengagement. *The Good Soldier Svejk* (Hasek 1973) is a novel about a Czech reservist recalled to the Austro-Hungarian army during the 1914–18 war. He was a disengager of heroic proportions, working his seemingly unintended depredations on the organization always from behind a mask of total dedication to the Emperor and to military life. He is the idiot of idiots, or so it first appears (that is the usual way in which his superiors address him), the complete fool, devoted to the military life but utterly incapable of getting anything done correctly. But soon it becomes clear that the army is the idiot, monumental in its incompetence, its officers unsurpassed in pomposity or stupidity or, in the case of Chaplain Katz, lechery and drunkenness. What the author wants one to think of the army and its officers is clear enough: the message constantly enjoins disrespect.[7] What he is saying

[5]I have taken *disengagement* from an essay by Azarya and Chazan (1987). It reverses a French word popular in the 1950s. *Engaged*, a term of approval, was applied to those who threw themselves wholeheartedly into public affairs, usually as vociferous protesters against established authority. I have given the word a more restricted meaning. My disengager, as will become clear, is neither vociferous nor an intentional "do-gooder."

[6]*Organizations* are groups created for a specific purpose, for example a business. *Institutions*, for example a family, are seen as ends in themselves. The attribution of moral status is a crucial distinction and will be discussed later. Where a cover noun is required I will use *collectivity*.

[7]The somewhat disorderly episodic construction of the novel not only reflects the fact that it was written as a series of short stories, but also,

about Svejk is more complicated. Svejk is not a fool; he only pretends to be one. Moreover, although usually in trouble, even in the worst misfortunes he has a proper regard for himself. There is no failure of nerve, no minimal self withdrawn and intent on nothing but survival, but an active calculating guardian of his own space, protecting his identity against organizational trespassing.[8] He lies and he cheats and he steals; but, I will argue, he is neither presocial (in "a state of nature") nor, in any absolute sense, antisocial. Svejk can be a moral person, but his morality does not always coincide with that of the organization that has him in its chains.

Svejk is not alone: few organizations—not universities, not churches, not armies, not the once supposedly regimented communist parties, and certainly not large industrial or commercial or civic enterprises—are without such figures, scheming, lying, stealing, using the organization's own resources to defeat its intentions. They serve *in* the organization without much serving it: scrimshanking, flanneling, swinging the lead, wangling, fiddling, dodging, and in many other ways using the weapons of the purportedly weak against those whom they see as would-be oppressors and exploiters.[9] The strategy is partly one of disinviting scrutiny, diverting attention from rule breaking or from an evasion of one's duties (as the organization defines duties), and concealing attitudes that incur official disapproval and therefore risk punishment. Alternatively, it is a way of showing disrespect for the organization by the ostentatious use of the organization's own proclaimed values, thus making it harder for the authorities to punish the offense.

Svejkism is a variant within a larger category of disengaging behavior, all of it subject to moral judgments. In one mode

perhaps, may be taken as an allegory of the author's own tumultuous life and his rejection of all regimentation. Hasek was clearly not a man of structure. See Parrott's introduction to Hasek 1973.

[8]Lasch 1984.

[9]All these terms refer to activities that benefit the individual and that the organization would consider cheating.

"disengagement" raises the question of privacy. At what point is it proper or feasible for an individual to refuse or otherwise avoid interaction with other people? It is also a question of boundaries: By what right do people of one social group mark the limits of their moral obligations by separating themselves from others, tribe from tribe or village from village? Third, disengagement can also refer to boundaries used by lesser groups to fence themselves off from the coercive attentions of a more inclusive group standing above them in a hierarchy: more exactly, from the attention of its officials. I am thinking of the way in which villagers whom I knew in India tried to keep at bay policemen, revenue officials, and politicians. Notice that in all these cases, an accusation of dereliction of duty would have to invoke one entity as privileged over another. Even in the first case, the privacy of the individual, an accusation of withdrawal implies neglect of duty and the collectivity's right to intrude with its demands.

At least seven features separate svejkism from other forms of resistance and identify its distinctive characteristics. First, svejkism always involves a conflict of moralities, a potential argument about where duty lies. Even the workers who steal goods or time from their employers could claim "cheating" in this way as their right, making up for exploitation. Second, the conflict is usually presented *not* as between rival obligations— time with my family against the demands of my job, or whatever—but as an individual's rights matched against the duties owed to an organization. In other words, one of the contestants is defined not as a moral person who has obligations to several collectivities, but as a rugged individual, standing alone and autonomous. This simple rhetorical construal, which is very common, has put some obstacles in the way of understanding what svejks do and why it is a mistake to write off every disengager as just another deviant.[10]

---

[10]I use "svejk" as a synonym for disengager. Where Svejk is capitalized, the reference is to the character in Hasek's book.

Third, whether we are talking of villages and officials in India, or peasants anywhere, or ethnic minorities, or individuals working in a factory, the interaction is always between unequals. By definition, Svejk's position is weak: the army has both power and authority over him.[11] He cannot use force to protect himself against exploitation; nor does he command the moral high ground occupied by a rhetoric of the public good.

Fourth, disengagement is not the same as open protest; it is either covert, concealed from the eye of the authority, or else it is camouflaged so that even though the authorities suspect its presence, they cannot easily take action against it. Its weapon is cunning; its style, when not hidden, is irony. Like jujitsu wrestlers, disengagers may use the organization's strength against itself; alternatively, they know precisely where to find its weak spots. They compete in that curiously elusive arena that is defined by secrets, open secrets, bluff and other forms of untruth, and messages that appear to say one thing but mean something different. Fifth, it follows that svejks are never reformers with conscious political intent, dissidents armed with programs of their own. A svejk's intention is not to change the status quo, but to exploit it as it is and to preserve a private space where the organization cannot intrude.

Sixth, to be successful at doing all that, and to compensate for lack of power, svejks must have minds that can operate beyond the thought limits imposed by the organization. They need the detachment that natural scientists are supposed to have, the capacity to see things as they are. This detachment is not a narcissistic withdrawal into the self, or into meditation on "higher" things. Rather it is cogitation, an active application of an independent mind to present problems.

Seventh, the organization is not only superior in power but

[11]A lowly person who maneuvers so as to take over an organization is not a svejk. A svejk certainly has ambitions to control his or her own space, but ambitions much beyond that are not part of the character. It is still possible, of course, that svejks in aggregate may substantially diminish centralized control. See Scott 1987.

also, by definition, intent upon exploitation. From a svejk's point of view all organizations are potentially coercive, either directly or through manipulation. The situation calls for self-protection through counterexploitation. Both the superior power and the evil intentions (and the necessity for deceit) are elegantly conveyed in a novel by K. C. Constantine (1983:13). Vinnie is a barman, talking about himself cheating his boss, and about the two of them cheating the government.

> Vinnie's argument was founded on something more durable than logic; there grew in his bones an unshakable knowledge of the systematic, organized, and foolproof ability of governments to screw the governed, which knowledge in turn inspired in him a duty to resist governments at every level by screwing them. To Vinnie it was all reduced to an emotion as close to patriotism as he could muster: America was great because where else could you cheat on your taxes the way you could in America? "You think I could get away with this kind of shit in Russia? Fuck those commies. Imagine a country where everybody's the boss, holy shit. . . . "

Evidently Vinnie finds it hard to imagine a working life without a boss. It is good svejkism, combining defiance with realism. Revolution would be foolish; the proper way is to "screw" the organization, and if everybody's a boss, no one's left to be screwed.[12]

If it were generally agreed that Vinnie's testimonial to hierarchy was quite wrong and that governments really are altruism in action, then not only Vinnie but also disengagers like Svejk would be recognized everywhere as evil. But they are not; indeed, often the inverse occurs. The svejks, lying, cheating, stealing, sabotaging the collective interest and—even worse—doing it apparently for their own advantage, may nev-

---

[12]The vast amount of "screwing" that seems to have gone on in Russia reveals "those commies" as less un-American than Vinnie thought.

ertheless be admired and, like Svejk himself, may become minor folk heroes.

How is this admiration to be explained? One could say that only bad people like Vinnie feel it, but that is not the case. Is it because we like self-reliance? Certainly in other contexts our culture unambiguously approves of self-sufficiency. Where the collectivity is thin and cannot provide the goods and services that are available elsewhere, we encounter pioneers, persons who pit their wits and skill against a hostile environment, and by their own efforts create an order out of the chaos. But, it must be said at once, pioneers do not defy a collectivity; they defy its absence. Svejk is defying a collectivity. Furthermore, pioneers are leaders, people who blaze the trail for others, and their triumph in the end is the creation of an ordered collectivity. Svejk is no leader, and he does not create order: usually he sabotages it.

Yet people like him. For some he may even become a role model, and even those who would not emulate his conduct are at least entertained by his exploits. He is not a great man, a hero like Napoleon. Nor is he an heroic dissident, like Gandhi or like Jesus, standing up for a principle against the might of an established authority, a David against Goliath. We admire heroic dissidents because we do not admire the institution that they defy and do not believe its claims to be a benevolent provider of order and good government. We see it as a trespasser into domains where it has no right to go, an exploiter, a predator, an enslaver, standing in the way of what dissidents usually call "the truth." For a dissident "truth" always turns out to be a better form of institution, one that will not be a predator and enslaver but the people's willing servant.

But that is not the vision of a svejk, the disengager. Svejks do not claim to represent some higher truth. I will argue that in their lives they do exhibit a certain kind of "truth"—they penetrate official pretenses—but they surely do not preach eternal verities. They are skeptical, inquiring persons, officially unimportant in the scheme of things, even in the organization that they serve (so long as they do their disengaging skillfully). They are reluctant servants, imprisoned in an organizational framework because they need the job, or because for some other reason they have no choice in the matter. The alienated industrial worker, the bored teenager determinedly not learning what the school purports to teach, the plantation laborer, and the unwilling military conscript are familiar examples of those whose lives are rendered drab and empty by the organizations that enfold them, and enlivened only if they learn how to be svejks and make themselves comfortable, materially and emotionally, by outwitting their masters.

Not everyone, however, admires svejks and their cheating. What svejks do obviously will not meet with their bosses' approval; for the bosses, anyone who does not respect authority becomes a symbol of evil, disruption, inefficiency, and of all those qualities that make life difficult. The attitudes of svejk's peers is less clear-cut, because they do not all have the same views on authority. First, there are some who have sold out and are on their way to becoming bosses; they are the non-heroes of a later chapter. Second, some (the proportion varying from one organization to another, or from one occasion to another) have been sufficiently brainwashed to lose their individual identity and submit to the organization's moral takeover. Both these categories see wickedness, or, at best, folly, in what a svejk does.

Third, I would guess that in most large organizations a majority among a svejk's peers is sufficiently detached from the organization to see usefulness—or even moral worth—*both* in loyalty to the collectivity *and* in disengagement. Svejk himself is quite close to this position, except that what he sees in the organization is mostly its usefulness. Fourth, there are some who, being sociopaths, lie and cheat and exploit, quite indifferently, both the organization and their fellow workers. They are not—I emphasize this—to be considered svejks, although the masters of the organization like to compound the two categories. Svejks have a somewhat offhand Robin Hood quality; in the main they are out to protect themselves, but not at the expense of their comrades.

The very common, if slightly cautious, approval for what a svejk does may spring ultimately from ideas about the essential immorality of power. Svejk is a symbol of resistance not just to authorities but to authority itself; he is not a revolutionary seeking to substitute a new authority for the one he undermines. Why should the implied anarchy be found admirable? It may be that deep in the popular collective consciousness is an idea of the perfect society—a demotic version of the philosophers' golden age, of life before the Fall, of the City of God, of Locke's benign portrayal of man in a state of nature. God's laws (or the laws of nature) provide a perfect design for social life. But the design is not realized and actual behavior is hopelessly corrupt. At first sight Svejk and his sort, the archetypical cheats, are the cause of this corruption. But this may not be so: perhaps the world is corrupt because the individual's access to God and to true morality is blocked by earthly rulers. Then it is the individual's duty, for example in Islam or in Protestantism, to follow God's rules and defy secular rulers, when they go astray.[13] The svejks that I have in mind would hardly justify themselves that way, except with tongue in cheek. But that notion of a higher duty could still give rise to a vague conviction that resistance to an earthly authority, when it is not done in the name of another earthly authority, may itself be a symbol of attachment to God's will.[14]

[13]This conviction that authority is the negator of spiritual values, and therefore inherently immoral, is well conveyed by some of the wartime writers quoted in Chapter 6.

[14]Thoughts about God I owe to Michael Meeker, then my departmental

Finally, svejks may be admired because they can outthink the organization and its masters. Even those people who are not the wholehearted disengagers that I have just portrayed, but are mostly satisfied with what they are doing in an organization and what it does for them, are likely from time to time to decide that they know better than their masters what has to be done; and on the quiet they do it. That, too, is a kind of disengagement. Svejk, in fact, is not so much a person as a mode of action practiced, at one time or another, by most people. What a svejk symbolizes for practitioners and other sympathizers is the thinking, cogitating self, valued because it is endowed with a capacity to transcend institutional orthodoxies.

In this case the rhetoric that justifies disengagement is not the rhetoric of resistance, of duty to a higher cause, as it is for a dissident like Gandhi, nor is it the remoter and more general rhetoric of obedience to God or to the laws of nature; instead it is the rhetoric of individual freedom.[15] This is not only freedom from material exploitation and regimentation, but also the freedom to have one's own opinions and one's own thoughts. Ultimately it is the capacity and the need for self-respect. Thus we arrive again at the far from simple notion of apparently autono-

---

chairman. The entailed structure of relations is certainly familiar: my enemy's enemy is my friend; old people conspire with their grandchildren against the middle generation; Caesar's allies in his battle with the Senate are the common people; and Presidents try to use the media (that is, the "American people") to keep Congress in its place.

[15]*Disengagement* better suits svejkism than would the in-vogue *resistance*. It saves me from having to make again Scott's trenchant argument against those who assume that "prepolitical" resistance is inconsequential until it is shown to lead to revolution. See Scott 1985: 289–303. Adas (1981) talks of *avoidance protest*. I have also heard *nonconfrontational resistance*. These phrases are mildly unsuitable because they foreground political motives and obscure what Vinnie the barman made clear: the essential banality of much everyday disengaging. Self-respect or money are the issues; not revolution.

mous individuals, thinking their own thoughts, exercising free will, and making decisions that are their own.

THE EXCESSES OF FORMAL ORGANIZATIONS

Why is disengagement a feature of organizational life? To say, economist fashion, that we disengage in order to look after ourselves, and to imply that looking after oneself and one's own interests is part of human nature, part of our genetic inheritance, may well be to speak the truth. But it is hard to demonstrate without begging the question, and in any case, it leaves a lot of experiences unexplained and a host of questions unanswered. We do not all of us, all of the time, disengage. Disengagement varies between different collectivities, between individuals in a particular collectivity, and between different occasions for the same individual. Moreover, examples of moral commitment are all around. If it is in our nature to disregard the interests of others, why do we so often not do so?

One answer is enlightened self-interest. We know that if we live by shafting others, sooner or later they will shaft us; so we behave with consideration for others. That answer also is sometimes true. But it seems to require a degree of enlightenment, and of constant calculation, that is implausible. Also it leaves entirely out of account the fact that most of these calculations, if they are calculations, are handed to us in the form of precepts, of preconceived opinions, rather than as the demonstrated results of some experiment. Does anyone ever look for a "proof" of "Do unto others as you would be done by"?

I will look for the source of variation in disengagement not so much in motivations (and not at all in psychodynamic explanations for motivational variation between individuals—that is a different kind of enquiry), but in the nature and activities of the formal organizations themselves, in particular those features which, from an individual's point of view, would be considered organizational faults. I will provide a brief anticipatory summary (amplified through the book) of an individual's view of these faults, for it is in reaction to them that individuals break "the crust of bureaucracy."

First, whatever they put out about themselves, organizations seem to have a poorly developed sense of right and wrong. Expediency all too often comes out ahead of morality. Organizations and institutions are supposed to be the guardians of trust and fair dealing, but often there is no one to guard the guardians, and—self-interest being a prime mover—they look after their own good rather than the public good. Of course, it is not a question of the organization having a moral sense; to look for an internalized morality in them is as sensible as expecting to find it in a computer. The lack of moral sensibility lies in the leaders and owners, who put their own advantage ahead of the common good, whether the good is defined as that of the society at large or of individuals. They do so behind a screen of respectability, of professed concern for the public good. Everywhere there is a major presentational effort either to deny self-interested behavior or to redefine it as altruism. Our motorcar is not unsafe at any speed, whatever consumer advocates claim to have demonstrated; another redefinition is the famous and ambiguous claim that "what was good for our country was good for General Motors, and vice-versa."

Second, organizations are given to excess. An organization that is minimalist in its intentions has to work hard to remain minimalist. The frequently heard joke about the university that wanted to cut down the number of committees and could only do so by appointing a further series of committees, one for each of its sectors and always in pairs, one to design and the other to implement the reductions, is an allegory reflecting the fact that organizations almost everywhere are intent on expansion, or at least on staying in business. In theory formal organizations should go out of business if they fail to perform the task for which they were set up. But failure, instead of terminating them, often is an incentive to indulge in other kinds of excess.

One is an excess of detail. Failing to be efficient, the bureaucracy gives more and more attention to detailed prescription of what should be done. This response is built into the very nature of a bureaucracy, which must try to anticipate every contingency and lay down a rule that will tell people how they should respond. In the end such attention to detail is counterproductive because the excessive weight of rules prevents anything being done at all. That is why "working to rule" is a way to harass an organization. That is also why the lower echelons of the Indian bureaucracy, certainly in British days and probably still, spent vast amounts of time and used vast amounts of paper to accomplish very small things. In time, those who work in such organizations lose sight of the task and transform the rules, making them not means, but ends in themselves.

To do this, they produce another kind of excess, a surfeit of organizational religion. If called into question, the ritualization of work and the ceremonial performances (like the military ceremonies which go on around the royal household in London) may be justified as ends in themselves or they may be justified instrumentally, as being necessary for the performance of the organization's task in the world. Othello's "pride, pomp and circumstance" (but without the "glorious war") raise morale, it is said, foster loyalty and dedication, and therefore make soldiers more efficient and more ready to serve. Alternatively, if in a particular case that argument is palpable nonsense, the apologists may change direction altogether, for example saying that the ceremony of Trooping the Colour in fact has nothing to do with military efficiency, but it is very good for tourism and for the balance of payments. Or it may be said that the performances are indirectly useful, as in the case of the aphorism attributed to the Iron Duke that Waterloo was won on the playing fields of Eton.

If the organization's task in the world is only to put on a show, then no harm is done. Professional soccer teams in Britain are there to perform every week and let people vent emotions and feel good or bad about the team's performance. But there are other situations in which sports teams, set up for recreation or entertainment, become ends in themselves and displace the organization's designated tasks, which is notoriously the case with team sports in some American colleges.

The principal problem is that both mindless adoration of the organization and an excessively detailed inventory of regulations have clear bad consequences for any organization that has a task requiring intelligence and individual initiative. Indeed, collectivities of every kind, both institutions and formal organizations, if they are set in their ways and iron-bound by their scriptures, are at the mercy of a changing world, for the true-believers have been schooled into not seeing or believing anything that the scriptures did not anticipate. In the same way, the absolute inability of the bureaucrat to foresee every contingency makes it self-destructive for an organization to eliminate the very capacity for independent critical thought that it needs to get its task in the world performed. In other words an excess of detailed regulation and an excess of organizational religion are faults that compound one another; both impede initiative and both contribute to disengagement.

Faced with an organization that manifests these excesses and is predatory in its demands, individuals may be prompted both to see themselves as individuals and to act that way. They may make an open rational protest, or rebel, or they may sink their individuality in one or another group of reformist or revolutionary activists. Such actions, I repeat, do not constitute disengagement. Disengagement aims to modify, but not to overturn, the existing distribution of power, to alter the pattern of exchange between those who command and those who obey. Disengagement may even be done with the good of the institution in mind. Disengagers, having decided that attempts at reform would be counterproductive, may adopt the covert way as the most efficient, in the interests not only of themselves but also of the organization. In other words, disengagement need not be total. One may disengage from the means while still accepting the ends; or one may quietly reject the ends, in some cases diverting the means to further ends that are not the organization's. Constructive svejkism occurs when rules about methods are disregarded so as to better achieve the organization's goals. It is a remedy for excessively detailed regulation. The other pattern of svejkism is the reverse: the organization's excess of regulations, or its ceremonial excesses, are used against it.

Just as organizational excess takes two main forms, so also does disengagement. The two forms are *symbolic* and *practical*. *Symbolic* disengagement, exemplified in carnival, is any kind of behavior that signals in a metaphorical way a refusal by the lowly to accept the identity that the authorities (and the conventions upheld by authorities) insist they should have. It is a grasping at self-respect. Symbolic disengagement is considered in the third chapter. Practical disengagement, the subject of Chapter 4, is an evasion of duties imposed by authorities, done in such a way that the authorities have no easy way to inflict punishment because they cannot find out who is cheating or how it is being done, or, indeed, if what is being done can legally be called *cheating*. Thus the offenders enjoy the benefits of being in the organization without having to pay all the dues that the organization wants them to pay. The rewards are material but often include enhanced self-respect. This type of practical disengagement, in the language of management, is called *shirking*.

What is it that individuals want when they disengage? The two modes of disengagement, symbolic and practical, are often combined in the one situation. When that happens scholars with an economic tendency subordinate symbolic action and treat it as epiphenomenal, a reflection of the underlying material reality, and mostly disregard it. But in fact an important part of reality is immaterial. Think of the bread and circuses that proverbially kept the Roman city mob contented, subsidized food and entertainment. From an economic point of view, popular discontent is then a function of the price of bread and the quality of the gladiatorial shows. That is indeed a simple formula for governing a city—the cheaper the bread and the better the show, the happier people are. But some finer tuning is appropriate.

First, the model suggests a trade-off between the price of bread and the price of admission tickets or the lavishness of the displays. If the harvests are poor or the supply ships from Sicily run into a storm and the price of grain rises, then it would be smart for the Roman authorities to put on a few gala performances in the arena. The point is a general one. Governments take the citizens' minds off present discontents by staging spectacular performances, such as exhibitions and festivals, witch-hunts for political protesters, show trials, organized pogroms of ethnic minorities, religious fundamentalism and its accompanying violence, or even by taking a nation into war.

But, second, the two parts of the equation—bread and the circus—are not of the same quality. Man shall not live by bread alone, St. Matthew tells us; one also needs the word of God. Circus is a very profane substitute for God's word, but the comparison suggests a closer look at what circuses did for the Roman mob that bread did not. Circuses satisfied some kind of nonmaterial need, which may not deserve to be called spiritual but certainly belongs in the domain of the psychological. That need is for identity; the need to be a person whose existence has meaning for others, who is recognized and respected, even if sometimes not liked. The provision of circuses acknowledged the ordinary citizen's right to be entertained, as a sentient being with aesthetic needs and standards (no matter how debased they seem now), as more than a mouth to be fed, more than an animal. That is what an entertainment does for spectators; they participate to the extent that they are given a sense of their own importance. A sense of selfhood may seem very immaterial when set beside a loaf of bread, but it is none-theless real.

This brief inventory of the excesses of formal organizations, of the needs of ordinary people, and of the two main forms of disengagement that emerge, assumes a calculating individual. In the next chapter I will look at the calculating collectivity. People who have their own opinions and think their own thoughts are often seen by those in charge as a threat to a collectivity. This threat may be contained by carrot-and-stick methods, reward and punishment. It may also be averted by persuading would-be independent thinkers that the organiza-tion (its owners and managers) is, like the condominium board mentioned earlier, morally entitled to decide for everyone what is good and what is bad, what can be done and what should be done; in others words, control may be exercised through hege-mony.[16]

[16]This word is in fashion and has several meanings. *Hegemony*, in this book, means that those who are ruled accept their own subjection as part of the natural order of things. Antonio Gramsci's ironic gloss is "'sponta-neous' consent" (his quotes. See Hoare and Smith 1971:12).

Chapter 2

Manufacturing Dignity

In [the English constitution] there are two parts (not indeed separable with microscopic accuracy, for the genius of great affairs abhors the nicety of division): first, those which excite and preserve the reverence of the population—the *dignified* parts, if I may so call them; and, next, the *efficient* parts—those by which it, in fact, works and rules. . . . Every constitution must first gain authority, and then use authority; it must first win the loyalty and confidence of mankind, and then employ that homage in the work of government.

—Walter Bagehot, *The English Constitution*

DIGNITY AND EFFICIENCY

Every formal organization, every bureaucracy, has Bagehot's two parts. "Efficiency" refers to the task it carries out, the job that it is designed to do; "dignity" is the domain of tradition, ceremonial, and symbolism. The mix of dignity and efficiency varies; some organizations concern themselves mainly with the symbolic domain (peacetime armies, Masonic orders, and the like); others are said to focus more on task than dignity (guerrilla bands, research teams, Smiley's people and other espionage organizations, the Department of Motor Vehicles, and so forth). But every organization has the two parts: dignity to win the loyalty and confidence of its members, thus motivating them; and efficiency, which is the use to which it puts that "homage" and its other resources.

Organizations are well aware of disengaging tendencies and invest resources in measures that will prevent them. There are two ways of doing so; one is by exacting compliance, and the other by engineering consent. Compliance is the product of rewards and penalties, and it signifies domination by the organization. Consent goes to an organization that its members consider legitimate; service is then a matter of conscience. Consent and compliance are theoretically in a trade-off relationship, compliance taking over where consent fails; the higher the consent the less the need for compliance. Enhanced dignity means enhanced consent, which may sometimes be cheaper than buying or exacting compliance and therefore an efficient way to use scarce resources.[1] This chapter is about consent and about the way in which collectivities attempt to manufacture devotion.

Among the several human dispositions that are said to be innate is "togetherness," a need to be with other people. If this idea is correct, all human beings are programed for sociability, which in its focused form becomes devotion to a group, and this propensity is the foundation on which devotion is manufactured. But propensities are raw material that has to be processed, potentialities to be cultivated like a flower from a seed. Also the propensity for togetherness is pointed in no particular direction, and an organization will benefit only if it can channel the sentiment in its own direction.

One way to do this is to promote a doctrine of holism, in which the institution is defined as the one true hope of salva-

---

[1]In practice most bureaucracies follow a fail-safe strategy of working for both consent and compliance. The trade-off between these two strategies, made necessary by limited resources, is examined in Chapter 5.

tion. An outright claim to divinity is unusual, but to talk of the organization's "mission" or its "destiny" is common enough, and certainly most organizations like their members to have god-fearing attitudes toward them. Moses said, "The Lord thy God is a jealous God." So it is with a god-posturing organization; if it has the power, it will not share its members with other organizations. Nor will it tolerate sentiments of individuality among its members. It will exact an imperative of depersonalization, the members being its instruments, supposedly having no identity outside the organization, the only valid self being "member." They are of use to the organization to the extent that other gods that might command their devotion— identities as father, mother, son, daughter, husband, wife, friend, enemy, Catholic, Jew, Protestant, Czech, Hungarian, the bearer of obligations outside the organization, and, not least, the rugged, resistant, resentful self—can be suppressed or at least made secondary.

In other words, every organization demands a measure of alienation. It does so, as I said earlier, with the intention of standardizing its members. Individuals alienate (that is, transfer or contract away to the control of another) a part of themselves, of their own identity, of the obligations they may have to other collectivities. That quasi-legal process, unless special countermeasures are taken, may result in a loss of self-esteem and, consequently, a *sentiment* of alienation, a feeling of estrangement or disaffection from the organization, a judgment that it lacks legitimacy. Alienation, as the *willing* surrender of autonomy by individuals, is much desired by organizations. But a sentiment of alienation negates legitimacy and makes service unwilling and is, from the institution's point of view, undesirable. Consequently institutions take pains to counter alienation by enhancing their own dignity.

Dignity? Bagehot's word, applied to individuals, means "true worth" or "merit" or "excellence." It is used also of someone who conducts himself with "proper stateliness." An institution's dignity is the measure of the awe, or at least the respect, with which it is regarded; the measure of how far it stands above doubt and criticism. Bagehot, writing in England in 1867 on the eve of an extension of the franchise, worried that representative government would be destroyed if the vote were extended beyond the middle classes. "I am exceedingly afraid of the ignorant multitude of the new constituencies" (1966:281; introduction to the 1872 edition). Good government was possible only through techniques that would arm the rulers with dignity and so make the masses respectful. I am extending the concept so that its magic works on anyone, not just on an "uncultured and rude population," and at the same time shifting its emphasis away from individuals (like the queen) or classes (like the aristocracy) in the direction of collectivities. I retain, however, the suggestion that domination must be buttressed by consent (ideas and attitudes) fostered by the authorities, sometimes cynically and sometimes because they too believe in the myths. Bagehot (and Plato) got to hegemony before Gramsci did.

Consent is fostered by means of rituals and ceremonies, the theater of collectivities. They are intended to stimulate a sense of devotion, diminish sentiments of individualism, and at the same time mark the collectivity's identity by differentiating it from other collectivities. Theatrical performances in an organization must also accommodate themselves to the fact that members come to them already formed by experience in the world outside, in particular with attachments to other collectivities. I will talk about soldiers, schoolboys, and people in universities, and I lead off with a random set of institutional poetic or theatrical performances in armies. They are drawn from experience during the 1939–45 war, while I was serving in the Brigade of Guards.

THE STIRRUP PUMP

In the corner of each barrack room at the training depot was a stirrup pump and a bucket of water, for use against incendiary bombs dropped in air raids.[2] To the pump was attached a length of black hose, about an inch in diameter. The bucket was painted white; the pump was painted black; the hose, which had a brightly burnished brass nozzle, was coiled neatly on the ground and its upper (visible) surface was polished with boot blacking until it shone like a dark mirror. Once in two weeks there was a fire drill, when everyone took a turn at manning either the hose or the pump, extinguishing a dummy incendiary. This drill was done outside. For these occasions all but the dumbest of squads had scrounged (acquired illicitly) a spare bucket and pump, so that the barrack-room set could remain immaculate, needing no more than the daily application of blacking and brass polish before the morning kit inspection.

Those pumps and the loving care bestowed on them, especially on the blackened coil of hose, were makers of dignity. They surely had nothing to do with efficiency, for continued disuse most likely dried out the valve inside the pump barrel. Not infrequently, military dignity and military efficiency came into collision. Three years later I watched a squadron of armored cars in Germany being prepared for a victory parade. The camouflaged green-painted aerials were cleaned with coarse emery paper, which stripped off not only the paint but also the copper coating, leaving the aerials bright and shining steel, and, without the copper, ready to rust and no longer of much use as aerials. Indeed, the sacrifice of efficiency was endemic, continuing even in wartime. At the training depots, squads always ran between classrooms; and before every course the instructor would explain that in the regular army they spent three months learning what we were about to learn,

[2]The stirrup pump was so called because at the end of a long bracket welded to the barrel (the barrel being placed in a bucket of water with the bracket outside) was a stirrup in which one inserted a foot to hold the pump steady while pumping the handle.

but now there was a war on, so we had to learn it all in three weeks. Time for training was clearly precious (this was a year before D-Day). But every Saturday morning, both at the first depot and later at Sandhurst, we marched past the commandant, squadron by squadron, a band playing, boots polished even down to the instep, belts blancoed, brass fittings gleaming, and performed intricate drill-square maneuvers that had their origins (and their most recent usefulness) on eighteenth- or early nineteenth-century battlefields. The rifle drills we learned for those occasions also, in many cases, were a couple of centuries old and had no direct application in battle. Indeed we once spent several hours, under a drill sergeant whose enthusiasm had run away with him, learning how to "rest on your arms reversed," a posture displayed by soldiers lining the route of a royal funeral cortege. All the time and effort spent in this way were an opportunity cost upon, time taken away from, training in how to aim and fire and maintain some fairly sophisticated guns, how to read maps, how to take advantage of the terrain, how to operate radio transmitters, how to maintain the armored vehicles, and in a thousand other ways how to function as an effective fighting force in mechanized warfare. Was all that antiquated and apparently purposeless ceremonial a waste of time?

If it was, then for many soldiers it was also an enjoyable waste of time. For some, it was not a waste of time at all, but the very essence of being a soldier. Undeniably, many were sucked in by the ceremonialism. They went at it with a relish that had nothing to do with the penalties that were inflicted on those who did not fold their blankets correctly, or failed to get a perfect crease in their heavy serge trousers. The triviality of it all did not diminish them, nor did the standardization. Quite the reverse; they felt empowered, confident in their collective excellence. They marched, even walked, with heads held high, feeling that they were the best that had ever been, could ever be. They were no longer the individuals they were before they

joined the brigade; in the context of excellence they never said
"I," always "we." True, it takes a very stupid person to feel
this way about blacking a fire hose, and that and similar rituals
usually provoked a mild derision (I will come to that later); but
if reprimanded for a less than perfect turn-out of the barrack
room and its equipment, squad members felt demeaned and
inadequate. It did not occur to most of them, at least after a
time, that the standards might be unreasonable or meaningless,
or themselves unjustly penalized.

In the conversion several things had been done to them.
First, they had learned the habit of blind obedience to the organization. Of course, the orders to be obeyed came from the
corporals and sergeants and officers, but, we were told, obedience to them was only an intermediate thing. In the end,
both the ordinary soldiers and those who gave them orders
were all alike subordinated to the institution; the army, the
brigade, the regiment, and so on down to the smallest *collective*
unit. Authority did not lie with any *individual*, not even the
mightiest. "You don't salute the man," we were told. "You
salute the uniform."

Second, inasmuch as the uniform counts and the man inside
it counts for nothing, is faceless, military rituals degrade the
civilian person. They do so in a very literal sense, removing all
the statuses that attached to a civilian at the time he joined the
service. The initiation rituals were very transparent. Men
stood in line for medical inspections, naked and undignified.
Civilian clothes were removed and replaced by a uniform. Everyone got the same toothbrush haircut. Recruits were spoken
to without respect, systematically abused and bullied, and they
eventually learned that safety lies only in the correct routinized
responses, delivered instantly, without hesitation and without
thought. Everything—words, clothes, attitudes, movements—
was uniformed. Then, one day the miracle had happened, degradation was complete, personal dignity had been destroyed
and its place taken by the faceless but very powerful dignity of

a uniform and of the collectivity; the spirit of true hierarchy was in command.

The completed transformation, third, produced not an individual who thinks and who is ready to criticize, but a diseducated automaton, which has learned, as David Lodge (1962) and several of Svejk's officers put it, to not-think (and therefore must be, to follow Descartes, a nonentity). But the not-thinker has feelings: a sense of belonging, a sense of devotion, a sense of fulfillment, of pride—good feelings, for sure, feelings that (a paradox) wonderfully inflate the ego, but are achieved at the cost of a mind. Evidence of this mental atrophy is the quite extraordinary capacity of soldiers, as I remember us, to sit still and do nothing for hours at a time, bored perhaps, but with a kind of passive boredom, an absence of restlessness that has in it no irritation and no urge to protest. The army, perhaps, had swallowed us so completely that when it had no task for us, we slipped into mental hibernation.

Those three effects—suppressing the critical intellect and elevating selected emotions, eliminating former obligations and concentrating loyalty on the institution, and instilling the habit of instant unquestioning obedience—constitute the acme of mindless consent and of institutional legitimacy. One instrument for bringing this about is ceremonialism, and the case of the military (at least as I remember it) is an extreme example. But it should be remembered that Svejk too was a soldier; evidently institutional theatrical performances do not always have the intended effect.

THE SCHOOL ASSEMBLY

Meanwhile, I will recount some experiences in a boys' school. The school had a far from meager ceremonial life, but was less ambitiously all-consuming of the individual than was the Brigade of Guards.

It was a day school, boys only, with about eight hundred pupils, supported by the city and at that time designated a "secondary" school.[3] Primary school education ended at fourteen. In secondary schools the leaving age for the majority was sixteen, but for a few education continued to eighteen, through three levels of the sixth form, in preparation for university entrance. The school had the technical status of a public school (the headmaster being invited to attend the Headmasters' Conference) and each year it sent a respectable number of its pupils (about twenty) to universities, of whom about half a dozen had won scholarships to Oxford or Cambridge. But the pupils were socially anything but "public school boys." Most of them came from working-class or lower middle-class homes, very few from professional families. For almost none of them was higher education a family tradition. The school was about seventy years old at that time, but I cannot recall a single schoolfellow in the sixth form whose father had attended the same school.

The school was housed in a substantial building, erected about the middle of Victoria's reign. It was five stories high, and had a facade of sandstone (smoke-blackened like every other building in the city at that time). It was built in the style of "Municipal Gothic"; pointed leadlighted windows, a form at once vaguely medieval and vaguely ecclesiastical, but with walls that ended fortress style in crenellations, thus adding a touch of "Scottish Baronial."[4] The school was fronted on the street, where the tramcars ran, by large ornate iron railings; the other three sides, surrounding an extensive playground, part cinder and part asphalt surfaced, were guarded by a twenty-five-foot high brick wall, topped with broken glass. Nowhere, in the entire place, was there a tree, or a plant, or a

---

[3]Some years later, following the 1944 Education Bill, the designation became "Grammar School."

[4]The architectural classifications are those of Sir Osbert Lancaster. See his *Pillar to Post.*

blade of grass. In short, architectural dignity up front, so to speak, (even if somewhat unconvincing) and, behind the Gothic facade, the plainest of plain utility. Interior walls were painted chocolate brown and dark green, and the lead-light windows made even the sunniest day somber inside the building. It could have been a prison; not, for sure, a promising setting for the invention of tradition and the manufacture of dignity.

On four of the week's six schooldays, a ceremony called "Assembly" was held in the school hall. The hall, appropriately, combined the features of a theater and a place of worship, and could accommodate all eight hundred pupils. It was octagonal, had two balconies, and a rusted tangle of iron fire escapes clamped to its outside walls. In one segment of the octagon, facing the body of the hall where the audience sat, was a large platform, like a stage, reached in front by steps on each side from the auditorium, or by passages in the wings. Behind the platform rose tiered choir benches, growing narrower to fit the shape of the hall, and reaching their climax in a large concert organ. The movements of the much-envied small boy designated to pump air for the organ could just be detected behind the tall gold painted organ pipes.

When they came to school in the morning, the boys reported directly to their classrooms (called "form rooms") and there, for all except the senior sixth forms, the form master called the roll. Then, down at the bottom of the stairwell in the center of the building, the school porter rang a handbell, and each form walked in Indian file to the hall, the form captain and the form master in his academic gown bringing up the rear. Each form went to its allotted section of the auditorium, and the master took his seat behind them. Seniority was indicated, roughly, by distance from the stage, the higher forms being further away. There was one exception to this order. The school prefects sat in the first row of the first balcony; they too entered in reverse order of seniority, the school captain being the last, taking his seat on the left of the aisle exactly in the center of the front row of the balcony.

When everyone was seated, the headmaster made his entrance from the wings (off side) and stood, in solitary grandeur, behind a large Victorian reading desk of the kind once used by clerks. It served as his lectern. When he entered the hall, the organ played, in a subdued fashion, and everyone rose to their feet, and remained standing until the headmaster gave the word to sit. There followed a brief, more or less Anglican, religious service. (There were no Roman Catholics among the eight hundred or so boys who attended in my time. The few Jews waited outside the hall, until the service was over, and then joined the assembly, taking their seats unobtrusively at the back.) The headmaster spoke the prayers, a couple of hymns were sung, and the prefects took daily turns to ascend the platform and read the lesson, using for this purpose a smaller lectern set off to one side. After the service, the headmaster made whatever routine announcements were needed. Sometimes there were special events to be reported: success at games, scholarships won to Oxford or Cambridge, the coming sports day, or the annual school play. Sometimes he used the occasion to speak strongly about matters that concerned the good name of the school: rowdy behavior on public transport, taking a proper pride in wearing the school uniform, the unfortunate prevalence of smoking among certain groups, the shocking discovery in the modern languages lower sixth of pornographic literature (which he called "smut"), and other matters of that kind. Once a week, we practiced choral singing. The ceremony concluded with the school song (in Latin and set to a somewhat hysterical Elgar-derived tune composed by the music master), and everyone marched out, reversing the order of entry; first the headmaster, then, from the balcony, the school captain, the prefects, the sixth formers, the fifth formers, and so on down the hierarchy.

The assembly was what now is called a "cultural performance." Its functions and its consequences are obvious: it made the collectivity, that is the school, visible and tangible, every morning to every boy who was present. Indeed, since this was a performance, deliberately staged, one can say that this was its purpose: to counter the fragmentation implicit not only in the six levels of forms, each with a further three or four grades within them, but also in the hourly shift from one classroom to another, and, beyond that, in the sharp division between classics, modern subjects, and science, and the even sharper division between those who were smart enough to compete for university admission and those who were not, and who would leave the school at sixteen to find a job—what later was called "streaming." For most boys both kinds of sifting began about the age of nine or ten.

The assembly was one of several devices intended to give the institution an identity and an importance in the minds of the pupils. The morning ceremony made visible not only the collectivity, but also its structure, its hierarchy. Assembly had very little to do with the business of the school, which was academic instruction. Success in that field was measured by places and scholarships won to universities, especially the Oxbridge scholarships. In that respect the school was like a university, a place in which to nurture individual intellectual talents, which is not primarily a collective activity. Scholars and schoolboys, therefore, are not faceless, like soldiers, whose function is almost entirely a collective one, entirely teamwork. In that respect at least, time at school was not like time spent in the army.

Nevertheless, the school went in for elaborate ceremonials, for uniforms (a prefect's cap had gold braid around the peak), and for other devices that have nothing directly to do with efficiency, but everything to do with dignity and legitimacy. For example, in addition to compulsory physical education in the gymnasium, there were also compulsory games (soccer, rugby, field hockey and, in the summer, cricket) played

Wednesday afternoons and Saturday afternoons. Teams for intramural competition were selected not from forms but from "houses." Each boy was allocated to a house on joining the school and stayed with it throughout. Houses carried the names of British battle heroes—Nelson, Drake, Raleigh, Wellington, and the like—and in a small way they set out to capture collective loyalties, holding fortnightly meetings that resembled the school assembly, having house captains and prefects, and so forth. Houses constituted a cross-cutting device intended to counter that form of inner-directedness (Riesman 1950), that ever narrowing focus, which is implicit in the academic subgroupings created by progress through the different forms, by academic specialization, and by streaming. The device was not very effective. In a boarding school houses are what the word implies, residential units, and therefore of importance in a boy's life. Ours was a day school and for most boys house affiliation did not much matter. Moreover, as in the case of military ceremonialism, the kinds of activity designed to promote collective sentiments were, from the point of view of efficiency, time wasters. Time spent on cricket, on singing hymns, or on punishing boys for failing to wear the school cap, was time that did not help win Oxbridge scholarships.

IMMUREMENT

Institutions take pains to give themselves an identity. One way of doing this is to mark, in some dramatic fashion, the boundary between themselves and the world outside.

Around the yard behind the school was the formidable brick wall, topped with broken glass. There was one truck-sized gate on the north side and one small door in the south wall, both kept locked, except when pupils were arriving or leaving. The main entrance was through a large terrazzo-floored atrium at the center of the facade on the west side of the school. It had imposing doors against the street and, fifty feet into the atrium, another barrier, consisting of tall ornate green and gold painted spiked iron railings, into which was let a gate. This too was kept locked during the hours of instruction, and the only way in or out led through an office at the side, where an unsympathetic lady entered the names of late arriving boys in a register, and would let no pupil out during school hours without an *exeat*.

There were several commonsense reasons for such arrangements. The school was in a rough neighborhood, which by the 1930s had become a slum; one had to think about security and the walls kept the local riffraff out. Alternatively, without locked gates, what check could there be on who came late to school? (Of course, there was a roll call in the form room, but that took place five minutes after the designated time of arrival.) Nevertheless the security arrangements, whatever the possible rationalizations, whatever their real functions, look to me now like symbols of incarceration. They told us, and everyone else, that we belonged inside, and that between nine and twelve noon, and one and four, there was no other world that need concern itself with us or be of concern to us.

The college I attended in Oxford, like all the ancient ones in the center of the town, fronted directly onto the street (with barred windows on the lower floor). The back, where the fellows had their private garden, was protected by a fifteen foot stone wall, topped with a hedgehog of revolving iron spikes. There were two quadrangles and two large gates, only one of which was in regular use. It was guarded by the porters' lodge. As I remember, the gates were closed at ten; one could gain entry by knocking, until eleven; entry after that meant a report to the college authorities. Alternatively there were three well-known and well-marked access routes over the walls, without much risk to one's neck, spikes notwithstanding. There were other ways in which our freedom was restricted. An overnight absence, discovered by the "scout" who brought a jug of hot water in the morning to one's room, would be reported and penalized. Again, one could entertain a woman in one's room (it was then an all-male college) between four and six in the afternoon; no earlier and no later. The porters kept check on this.

Here too it is easy to find practical reasons for the symbolic (and actual) confinement. The architecture was a hangover from the fourteenth century and later periods, when walls and gates were a practical necessity. In addition there was a clerical heritage from the time when all university teachers were in holy orders. We lived in a walled community, and, being antecedently celibate, had no legitimate converse with women. There was also the college's obligation to protect the souls of its students from temptation and their bodies from harm; the college was *in loco parentis* and the students were *in statu pupillari.*[5] The symbolism of enclosure, of protection from the world outside through immurement, was quite obvious.

The army did it too. One of the training depots was a late-eighteenth-century building, complete with walls like a college. The other—a hutted camp—was relatively modern and much expanded in wartime, and the owners had to make do with a barbed wire fence to mark the boundary. Both institutions had a single main entrance, which was highly ritualized; always spick and span, a lawn and a flower bed edged with white painted rocks, a low white fence, a flag (to be saluted as one walked by), a sentry on duty, and that navel of the *corpus militare*, the guardroom (also called the "clink"). That was the only official way in and out of the depot, and one was required to show a pass, leaving and entering. As with the college, there were several clandestine ways of getting in and out, and the ceremonial of the main entrance was just that, more a matter of dignity than of efficiency.

Incarceration does seem to concentrate emotions on the insti-

---

[5]The Latin *pupillus*, from which we get *pupil*, means *orphan* or *ward*.

tution. "Day boys," who live at home and therefore have outside contacts, have a diminished standing at schools where
most of the boys are boarders; they are not wholly "of the
body." Boarding schools and Oxbridge colleges are better at
fostering unthinking devotion to the "old school" than are day
schools or commuter universities. Books that demolish the leg-
end of school as "the best days of your life" are seldom written
by people who went to day schools, because those schools lack
the python capacities of boarding schools, and are usually unable to stimulate devotion to the level where it provokes contradiction. The same is true of commuter colleges compared with
residential colleges.

The principle works from the other direction too. If contact
with outsiders is experienced as painful and involves rejection,
organizational solidarity is likely to be enhanced. Any institutional occupation that puts a barrier between the agent and the
outsider client, will tend to create a sentiment of solidarity and
a mythology of institutional distinctiveness. The barrier may
be one that arises from the contact itself, as in the case of policemen, who are resented because they exercise an everyday
and generalized authority over others. The barrier may also be
created simply by a sense of being different. Schoolteachers are
not like ordinary people because they work with children and
have responsibility for other people's children. They acquire a
sense that they are special and have a vocation, which is absent
in the case of, say, window cleaners or sheet-metal workers. It
does not, of course, follow that schoolteachers automatically
exhibit unthinking devotion to their own ideology and to the
collectivity. The situation is more complicated than that, and
Mr. Chips is probably not the modal figure in the profession.
The requirement to use their minds pushes many teachers in
the direction of individualism and institutional skepticism. But
when they decide they are held in low esteem and rewarded
less than they think right, as often happens in the United
States, they become ripe for institutional true-belief; they more

readily see themselves as a collectivity that has not merely interests but also moral standing.

The link between high walls, which exclude contact with others outside the organization, and a mind fully occupied by the organization can be made even in the case of prisoners in jail. "Devotion," of course, is not an appropriate word; but "mindlessness" is. Routines of systematic de-individualization, inflicted upon soldiers in armies and patients in some hospitals, reach their extreme in the case of convicts. Compliance, achieved through the threat of punishment and some meager rewards, is helped out by excluding all relationships that might mark the prisoner as anything but a prisoner; the goal is to make "convict" an entire identity, to define an inmate as a person without the capacity for any other role, and consequently to stifle any desire to take initiatives.

OUTSIDE THE PALE

Dignity, to judge from the tactics which would-be total institutions follow, can be achieved only through a zero-sum contest. The institution's dignity is won at the cost of degrading both other institutions and individuals. The world outside the group is presented as inferior, living without morality, and probably therefore dangerous. The message, conveyed through stories and symbols and performances, gives "us" our identity by telling us what others are like: the message is always that they are not like us and usually are best avoided. Walls, in other words, can be built with symbols. As the metaphor of "walls" suggests, the difference is rarely benignly perceived: it carries a varying measure of rivalry, of conflicting interests, and of potential domination. Difference, in short, is marked in this context as between good and bad, high and low, strong and weak.[6]

---

[6]That these judgments are reversed in the case of convicts demonstrates that, for their inmates, prisons operate at the minimal level of dignity.

The belief that the outsider has magical powers and is malevolent is common; it may be employed to frighten children into behaving themselves and to give them the sense that safety lies only within the community or the family. A similar idea, that the other person is dangerous or ridiculous or without moral feelings, less than human, is manifested in racism, class prejudice, and sexism. But in the case of institutions and formal organizations there is one very distinctive feature. The "others" are not real strangers, not unknown, and not even so very different from "ourselves." Institutional units—villages, schools, regiments, or universities—are very like one another in basic form and function, and it is usually the closest and most similar institution that has to be marked off and defined as something outrageously different. From the long view one regiment is much like another, one school is much like another, and that would be perfectly obvious if schools and regiments did not take so much trouble to make themselves distinct. Any such collectivity asserts, as an indisputable fact, that it is unique, but at the same time, somewhat illogically, works hard to make itself seem so; to make itself one of a kind, distinct from any others; to make sure that the principle of holism stops at its own boundaries and is applicable nowhere but to itself (which is, of course, perfectly logical, because two or more all-encompassing entities cannot coexist).

Sometimes institutions use small and relatively benign markers of difference. I was for a time puzzled, and then rather bored, by a succession of people in Valdieri, a village where I lived in Italy, who, uninvited, would give me a list of dialect words unknown in Valdieri but current in Entracque, a place about two miles further up into the mountains. "We say *cantina* but they say *sella*," followed by five or six more examples. Then I realized that I was being educated. I might have had the impression that, since the two villages were about the same size, were both head villages of their communes, both had parish churches, and both used the same three languages (Italian, Piedmontese, and the Nicois dialect), and were both in something of an economic decline, Valdieresi must be more or less interchangeable with Entracquesi. My unsolicited vocabulary lessons were intended to undo that impression. They did so by magnifying minute and trivial differences.[7]

The same is true of soldiers. Regiments have a room at the regimental depot that serves as a shrine for ancient pennants (regimental "colours") and weapons and uniforms and drums and bugles, and portraits of old colonels and paintings of battles long ago. Regiments celebrate victories, but they do not celebrate the entire event so much as their own part in it. In the battle of Waterloo the regiment took part in a cavalry charge; the battle also happened to mark victory in the Napoleonic wars, but that is incidental. Uniforms, for quite practical reasons, are different as between cavalry and infantry; but the uniforms of both cavalry and infantry regiments are further made distinctive by badges, by the cut of the tunic, by the number of buttons and their arrangement, and a vast and ingenious assemblage of diacritical marks that serve no practical purpose except to make clear that what might seem to be just another regiment is really one of a kind. Less formally, every regiment has a set of stories about other regiments, most of which are intended to do them no credit: about heroes who in reality were less than heroic, about traditions that are spurious, about origins that are contested (Which was the senior regiment of foot guards, Coldstream or Grenadier?[8]), and (more entertaining than questions of seniority) a surprisingly common mythology about sexual perversions and regimental mascots (usually a goat), and a variety of other scabrous inventions. These were passed on to us, as recruits, in rare moments of relaxation, by the senior NCOs.

Our school was not like the Roman Catholic boys' secondary school (of about the same size and academic standing) that

---

[7]A similar particularity is described for New Guinea in Schwartz 1975.

[8]Not coincidentally, the motto of the Coldstreams is: *Nulli Secundus*— Second to None.

faced it, also behind high walls, across the road. We all knew that they were not like us, and the school itself did not need to mount any particular cultural performances or to develop a specific mythology to mark this difference. The larger community did the job in a way that was the source of much civic distress. At that time, in that city, no one needed to be told that Catholics and Protestants were different kinds of animal. The customary riot that took place every year on Orange Day made the distinction very obvious. (The riot usually began about half a mile down the hill from the two schools, when a Catholic half-brick silenced the Orange Band's big drum.) There were, as I said, no Catholic boys in our school, and, so far as I know, no Protestants over there. The reason for this division had to do with more than what kind of religious instruction was given in the classroom. It was a matter of closed moralities, the implied assertion being that the good life was not possible outside this one particular and unique collectivity. To belong was to be sheltered from the bad life, from evil. That same fanaticism, that same true-belief, is the logical end of all those cultural performances and myth-making, whether regimental or in schools or in colleges. Fortunately for the world, the logical end of true-belief—the triumph of holism— is not so easily attained: unfortunately, it sometimes comes very near to being attained.

Similar performances are to be found in universities. I had the good fortune to teach for seven years in a new university in Britain, at a time when material resources were more plentiful than they are today. In the university's official philosophy, however, material resources took a bad second place to human resources. By "good university men" (females too could qualify) our leaders meant not the intellectual brilliance of the professors and the lecturers, but rather their unlimited willingness to go as many extra miles as was needed to make the institution the radiant success it was advertised to be. We were indeed brainwashed into seeing our institution as unique.

The university's "owners" were at great pains to make it distinct from other places, with which the untutored might confuse it. (I explain "owners" later. In the meantime, think of them as those who decided what kind of place the university was going to be.) The lesson that was given to me when I joined was, first, that the education of undergraduates was the central activity, and that the model for this was how things were mainly done in Oxford and Cambridge: by tutorial teaching and in small seminars. This system was both possible and desirable, the owners said with quite unashamed elitism, because only the most able students would be admitted (comparable to the best of those who went to Oxford or Cambridge). Second, the curriculum was of the type that in the United States is called "Liberal Arts" and was explicitly designed to avoid early specialization. One drastic measure was the elimination of departments; scholars in any one discipline would be attached to (and physically located in) different "schools." Students took their B.A. in a discipline (sociology, physics, economics, history, geography, whatever) but only six of the twelve courses taken in the three undergraduate years were in that discipline. Of the rest, four were selected from each school's distinctive smorgasbord of "contextuals," each of which was taught by a team of lecturers from at least two different disciplines (thus stepping around the trap of early specialization, albeit sometimes at the cost of intellectual coherence). Furthermore, *everyone* on the Arts side took the same two preliminary courses in their first two terms: one in history and the other in philosophy. (The remaining first year course was an introduction to the major subject.) The corresponding arrangement on the science side of the university was less liberal, as one would expect, all the courses (in those early days) being physics or chemistry or mathematics or biology, while a contextual was simply a course given under the rubric of one of the other major subjects. The scientists were not much impressed by the founding ideology and were somewhat reluctant to delay or dilute specialization. They already had their own commonality in certain specialized technical skills (such as calculus) that are required of science students everywhere.

In other words, scientists notwithstanding, the university professed to have a single unified philosophy of education as the center of its identity. The owners called it "a new map of learning," but in fact this philosophy was neither new nor unknown elsewhere, although the administrative framework for its implementation (such as eliminating departments) was certainly not common. That we did have our own distinctive ideology was forced home to us by frequent reference to negative examples. These were generically known as "Germanic"; too much and too early specialization, a concentration on research, large lecture courses, remote teachers, and a curriculum in which specialized disciplines had squeezed out the essential part of a "true" education, which is discourse about the eternal verities. If "Germanic" seemed too general, the preachers pointed a specifying finger at London university and the nineteenth-century provincial universities (Birmingham, Liverpool, Leeds, and the like), as good examples of what we were not going to be. We were not there primarily to advance knowledge; our task was to disseminate wisdom.

The diacritical exercise was not done indirectly (as with distinctive uniforms for soldiers or schoolboys), but by more or less straightforward assertive propaganda, both within the institution and beyond it. We told each other how different we were from the rest; and for a time the tabloid newspapers played along with a mild travesty of our distinctiveness, presenting the university as a "fun" place at which to get an undergraduate education.[9]

Words rather than pageants and material symbols, quite ap-

---

[9]The popular image was to some extent helped in the early years by the presence of some well-connected and distinctly eccentric undergraduates, and by the fact that metropolitan journalists were only an hour away by train.

propriately in a modern university, were the standard medium for cultural performance. There were two exceptions. The university, although of recent foundation, had concocted a totally medieval degree-giving ceremony, engaging the royal dress designer to create gowns and hoods (including a wonderful outfit for those of decanal rank, complete with biretta, which made several of them who were stout and had five-o'clock chins[10] look like Charles Laughton playing the part of an unsavory Sicilian bishop).

Second, the designers of the place did not neglect to use architecture to deliver messages about the institution's intellectual structure. The philosophy of the place—non-"provincial" and non-"Germanic" and no departments—was written into the buildings. The conventional difference between Arts and Science was marked (reluctantly, I assume) by locating them on different sides of a wide stretch of turf that ran like the fairway on a golf course from the entrance to the back of the campus. On the east side lay the single school that at that time represented science, the School of Physical Sciences. In fact it had separate buildings for Physics, Chemistry, and Biology, each of which later became schools in their own right—in effect, super-departments. This dividing turf was symbolically quite appropriate (but unintentionally so, I imagine) because the science side of the university bracketed away the "liberal arts" philosophy and went its own way (which was in the direction of specialization).

On the west side of turf, the different schools (Afro-Asian studies, European studies, Social studies, English-American studies, and various others) either had their own buildings or were located in distinct parts of a building. Somewhere near the center of each school's cluster of offices was a common room, shared by faculty, undergraduates, and the few graduate students enrolled in those early years. Adjoining offices were

---

[10]Elsewhere called the Nixon shadow.

occupied by teachers of different disciplines—my neighbors were from economics, political science, geography, and history, and the next anthropologist was way down the corridor (there were other anthropologists in other buildings). This arrangement symbolized our distinctive pattern of segmentation and the high value set on cross-disciplinary (that is, non-specialized) studies.

With those two exceptions, the university marked its structure and its unity with symbols that tended to be less blatant than those of schools or regiments because they were ostensibly not ceremonial. Indeed, much of the cultural performance was quasi-cerebral, a play that hid the substance of poetic performances behind the prosaic mask of efficiency.

If architecture was used to symbolize our distinctive pattern of segmentation, the theatrical performances that denied fragmentation and brought us together, marking us as one mind and one body, were committee meetings. These addressed the institution's need to indoctrinate its faculty, who had all come to it from elsewhere, some even from "Germanic" fellow-travelers like provincial or American universities. Several messages, which are quite unlike those of the army, were being transmitted through committee rituals, reinforcing the straightforward propaganda about our "new map of learning."[11]

The prime subliminal message was that these occasions had all to do with efficiency and nothing to do with dignity. Committees, one was led to assume, had a job to do; they were not time wasters, as in so many other places. They made decisions without which the university could never fulfil its task of guiding the young through the territory defined by the new map of learning. In fact they were just like committees anywhere—a range from a few elite ones that really did have power to others

---

[11]"Mindlessness" and "not-think" would have been unmentionable, although in fact such conduct was not unknown. See the later discussion of a dean and GUMs.

that existed only so that someone could say one of the two things that are said about committees: *We need to ascertain the general opinion* or *A committee is meeting to consider the matter.* But, in conformity with the university's image of its own uniqueness, our committee system was considered different. Even the common academic grouse that committees are a waste of time was somewhat paradoxically exploited, and committee work was programed in a way that connoted efficiency. Throughout the university (with a few exceptions), committees met only on one day of the week. This meant that for many of us, nothing much else was ever done on a Wednesday. But it was considered a mark of efficiency to schedule meetings that way, presumably because it left four working days on which time need not be wasted in committees.

But there were messages within messages. The fact that decisions were ostensibly being made by a committee and not by an officer of the university (or at least not by them alone) was itself a performance that celebrated the collectivity. These were activities that made us part of "the body." These committees in some ways resembled the school assembly or even what was done on the army's drill square. The meetings were exercises in participation, giving the sense not only that one was "of the body," but also just a little in charge of it. This was self-government, we could say to ourselves, not the exercise of power from on high. But those on high often did exercise power. This was usually done out of sight, but I do recall one meeting in which the chairman, a dean, provoked a walkout by refusing to divulge the information on which he based his insistence on a particular decision. Moreover, as in most formal organizations, large committees tended to demean themselves by attending to trivia in a way that made one wonder whether "self-government" was worth the trouble. One senate meeting discussed (among other things) these three issues. First, flints were working through to the surface of the rugby field and there was a danger of players disemboweling themselves in a tackle. Second, the municipal transport service between the university and the town (where at that time most of the student residences were located) left much to be desired. Third, it had been reported that our students—boys and girls—were having carnal knowledge of each other in the residences. The senate tied itself in knots debating the principle involved in the last issue. Its elders, heavy men with a strong sense of institutional responsibility, were not much amused when someone suggested bicycles were the answer: exercise in place of rugby, own transport, and no energy left for fornication.[12]

Third, since the nonspecialist committees that involved ordinary members of the faculty (like the academic boards or the senate or the general meeting of a school) were large, there was much opportunity for sounding off, and that meant celebrating the principles on which we were supposed to make decisions and denigrating their opposites as Germanic or provincial.[13] The senate in particular was an occasion for this kind of rhetoric. (I had lost the knack of mental hibernation acquired in the army, and meetings seemed interminable. I sometimes wondered if the chairman kept them going because otherwise he would feel obliged to go home and read a book.) There were also, of course, many equally impassioned speeches about how we were *not* fulfilling our mission.

Our mission never was fulfilled.[14] Some years later management consultants were called in (on whose initiative I do not know) and their recommendations made the place more like the

---

[12]Universities, at that time, still saw themselves *in loco parentis*. This was exactly the issue when the senate debated what should be done about copulating students.

[13]Specialist committees are those charged with a narrow and specific task: examinations boards, the library committee, student discipline committee, and so forth.

[14]It was a good university at that time, giving a good education, even a good "liberal" education. I mean only that the much publicized ambitions, which so excited people like the deans or the vice-chancellor, were rarely fulfilled, and even when fulfilled they did not hold for long.

other universities, raising its rating in the league table of research on the arts and social science side (hard science had done fine from the beginning). Then the sixties revolution overtook the place. Deans were no longer appointed but elected, and they held office for a limited period. They were often junior. Several of the founding fathers, guardians of the hierarchy, departed for Oxford or Cambridge or North America, and power supposedly flowed down the hierarchy, but, as one would expect, in fact much of it fell into the hands of the professional administrators. Finally came the Thatcher era, and I hear little now of liberal-arts adventuring in that place. Nor, the survivors say, is there much left of the rhetoric of nonpareil.

APPROPRIATING DEVOTION

No formal organization, not even a school, starts with raw material. The people recruited are already shaped by other experiences, and most of them already know what loyalty is. Therefore it is sometimes possible for an organization to appropriate devotion that had been directed elsewhere. There are several ways of attempting this usurpation.

Stealing through metaphor is the cheapest. Value-laden terms that draw their strength from organisms or from more "natural" institutions are appropriated. Some metaphors are bold and still enough alive (even if archaic) to catch one's attention: "of the body" as a persuasive substitute for "a member of the organization."[15] Family metaphors, on the other hand, are so frequent that they either slide by unnoticed or else acquire the patina of irony: brothers-in-arms, mother church, *alma mater* for a school, and the like. Parent/child, connoting nurturing and shaping and forming, stands for collectivity/individual. A

---

[15]"Member" (from *membrum*, a limb or part of the body) is, as a metaphor, quite dead.

child of God, or of the Revolution, or of the Sixties, or of anything else, is a person who has thoroughly and completely internalized those particular values.

For various reasons more direct appropriation of existing sentiments of moral commitment—examples are given below—are rarely effective. The predatory organization's integrity is diminished because the members are reminded that they have, or had, other allegiances, and they may even be reminded of sentiments that still can direct their loyalties elsewhere. This danger exists even where there are no attempts at appropriation. All formal organizations, while insisting on their own integrity and uniqueness, in fact must adjust themselves to surroundings that contain alien values, some of which aid the manufacture of organizational devotion, while others get in the way.

First, some organizations are framed by larger units into which they are formally incorporated. Despite the need to mark distinctiveness, described earlier, each level of an organization sets at least a basic ideological pattern for the level below it. The regiment is within the Brigade of Guards, and the Brigade is within the army, and the army is part of the armed services. The school is one of several secondary schools, grouped under the city's department of education, ultimately under the national education system. The college is part of the university, and the university is part of a larger national organization concerned with higher education. This arrangement is one reason why regiments and schools and similar collectivities strive to present themselves as unique.

The distribution of basic ideologies through an organization is complicated, and, as one would expect, influenced both by the task each unit has to perform and by its standing. Oxford and Cambridge for many years held themselves aloof from other universities; the new university worked hard to make itself distinct; universities and polytechnics in Britain do not (or did not at that time) occupy the same educational space. But, at some level of generality, even if sometimes quite vacuous, they must all share attributes that define higher education. The same is true of soldiers: the task of the Intelligence Corps separates it from the infantry, but even the Intelligence Corps cannot avoid some measure of the mindless obedience that characterizes military life, and, even in the Pay Corps, recruits learned how to fire a rifle. But the transcending ideology, like the waters of the Nile, seems often to vanish into the sands as it trickles downwards, and—a change of metaphor—to be trumped by other narrower loyalties.[16]

Second, formal organizations live in the context of "communal" institutions, such as families, villages, neighborhoods, ethnic groups, and nations, which in comparison are privileged by having *ab initio* a moral status. These institutions are sometimes caught in a zero-sum game with formal organizations. They already own what a formal organization wants, and they are perceived as obstacles in its way, when it tries to manufacture devotion for itself. An obvious example is family obligation. The peasant family "gives" (and thus loses) a son to the priesthood; the priest may not take a wife and have a family of his own. Regular officers in the British army, almost up the Second World War, had to seek their colonel's permission to marry if they were less than twenty-eight years old. Men of Shaka Zulu's regiments, recruited by age, were bachelors until the king "retired" them and they could find brides among a regiment of girls, similarly retired. Schoolboys, at least in the cohort to which I belonged, sacrificed much of their life in the neighborhood peer group, and were often somewhat distanced from their families, even when the latter were supportive.[17]

---

[16]Among other things this book is an attempt to find out why would-be pervasive ideologies fail to communicate themselves effectively down as far as the svejks. The subject, however, is too large to be treated comprehensively here.

[17]The same principle—rivalry for devotion or for respect—is at work when a group that has demonstrated moral solidarity by defying authorities is then dispersed by the authorities. That happened to the Cuban

But outright denial is not the only route. Sometimes the sentiment of affection for a moral community is considered fungible, so to speak, and the organization tries to cash in by appropriating a ready-made devotion. Some Oxford colleges had regional affiliations, but in my time this had little to do with devotion to the college. The school that I described, since it was a day school, drew all its students from the same city. But local loyalties (notably to the city's two rival professional soccer teams) were conspicuously excluded both by the school and by the city's authorities.[18] The army, however, made a big thing of regional loyalties.

For many years most regiments in the British army were locally raised, bearing names that indicated their origin, and having a depot in the region: the South Lancashire Regiment, the Northumberland Fusiliers, the Cheshire Yeomanry, the Middlesex Regiment, the Liverpool Scottish, the Sussex Yeomanry, and hundreds of others. Even in the two world wars, when the chaos caused by casualties and conscription tended to randomize the allocation of replacements, regiments continued to maintain local affiliations, thus, it was hoped, implanting in the soldiers that kind of unthinking loyalty and sense of comradeship that is the privilege of kith and kin, of neighborhood and community and family. Quasi-ethnic loyalties also were used, as in the case of the Royal Scots or the Welch Regiment or the Black Watch or the Argyll and Sutherland Highlanders; and the Foot Guards include Welsh, Irish, and Scots Guards. I can think of two instances in which even a vocation was put to use: the Artists' Rifles and the Inns of Court Regiment (lawyers).

---

detainees who mutinied and took temporary control of their American jail; when the group was subdued, the members were scattered over different jails. Their solidarity had to be destroyed because it diminished official authority.

[18]All the city's secondary schools competed in an annual soccer "Shield" competition. The final was played alternate years on the ground of each professional team.

To some extent formal organizations may benefit from the fact that people recruited into them already know what it means to feel obligation, if not to give devotion, to a collectivity. Then all the organization has to do, one might suppose, is redirect the sentiment toward itself. It would then follow that the creation of organizational devotion should be easier in societies, like Japan, where the people are more or less innocent of rugged individualism (at least as they are presented in current popular writing). Contrariwise, organizational devotion should be very difficult to foster in nations like Australia or any American state that has a frontier tradition, where individuals are expected to go their own way. If you need evidence for this proposition, it might be said, ask yourself who goes on strike more often, the Japanese or the Australians.

But generalizations like that, drawn from the business pages of the newspapers (for the Japanese) and from the folklore that Australians like to put out about themselves (a nation of vociferous individualists, contemptuous of authority in all its forms), remain very much in doubt. The facts themselves are in doubt because they have been impressionistically gathered. Furthermore, if they are facts, they may not be about devotion and consent at all, but about compliance or noncompliance. It may be that inside every Japanese employee is a frustrated svejk, and the only difference between them and the Australians is that Australians manage to let it out (and are applauded by their peers for doing so).

The other difficulty is that the immediate transference of "national character" into organizational behavior is an intellectual maneuver that is too cavalier. This is not to say that the concept of national character is inappropriate; but it is to say, first, that one must watch for the propagandist element, the possibility that the purported character is nothing but talk and never emerges in action, and in itself is not enough to account for the way people behave. Second, *national* character may be qualified by regional or class affiliations and cannot be taken alone as a variable influencing behavior in formal organizations. The same is true in the case of locally recruited regiments.

The main intervening variable both in the Australian case and the army's regiments is class affiliation. Putting it simply, each nation (Britain or Australia) is Disraeli's two nations, having a dominant class and a subordinate class. Each of these classes may have a different character; then there would be not one national character, but two. Or, if there is an encompassing character, covering both the dominant and the subordinate classes, it may have nothing much to do with the way people conduct themselves. See what happens to the untamable individualism of the Australians, when class becomes a factor in the equation. Australians present themselves as vociferous individualists and boast about their proclivity for disaffection from authority. But when the dockers refused to load ships carrying arms for a colonial war in Indonesia, they were not individualists at all; they were good union men, who were going on strike for a principle, for an ideology, out of loyalty to a socialist collectivity. In other words, they were activists, supporting a cause, labor, that saw itself in fundamental opposition to management, to capitalists, and to the government of the day. Where was Australian individualism in this? This was not a case of rugged individualism; rather it was a clash of ideologies. A plain statement, attributing labor troubles on the Australian docks to a purported Australian national characteristic of liking to be no man's servant, would be less than accurate.

The case of the locally raised regiments, hoping to subsume regional loyalty and comradeship, is more complicated. Certainly the outcome, insofar as it was a failure to manufacture devotion, had something to do with class feelings. But it also had to do with another and related feature of industrial society: specialization.

My memory is that the relatively specialized military units, artillery, engineers, signal corps, tank corps, marines, ordnance, service, pay corps and so on, were less inflected by the idea of the officer as gentleman, than were regionally based infantry and cavalry units; certainly less so than Guards units which were firmly hooked into the quasi-feudal mystique of the monarchy. The image in specialized formations leaned more toward the officer as expert. The relative absence of ritualized attitudes of snobbery in specialized formations arises, of course, from the specialization itself, which cannot permit the highly developed stupidity that goes along with ritually induced automatism. But it also came, I suspect, from the fact that most such units (not all) were recruited randomly with respect to region, and did not carry into the service acceptance of local class-based divisions and, especially in the case of rural areas, the almost feudal attitudes of deference to the upper class that still existed between the wars in some parts of Britain.

Troopers who had been hunt servants, farm laborers on country estates, or the sons of small farmers in the shires, or tradesmen and clerks and craftsmen from the same areas, brought into the army a ready-made habit of more or less unthinking deference to the officer class, and the holistic frame of mind that goes along with such deference. Factory workers, urban-based artisans, and the like, did not; they came armed with suspicion about the bosses and with the habit of thinking that anyone who gave orders was a kind of foreman, could not be a friend, and did not deserve trust, let alone devotion; *a fortiori*, neither did the organizations that such people managed. Given that the vast majority of people in Britain live in cities and work in the industrial economy and have done so for a century and more, this problem also existed, at least potentially, in the peacetime regular army. But then there was time for conversion, for the organization to remake the mind-set of its soldiers, and to teach them the virtues of consent and the comforts of unthinking compliance. But the citizen army could not do that. In the war there was not enough time; and the raw material, so to speak, was not the same. Those who joined the wartime army, whether volunteer or conscript, were not programed for a lifetime military career.

The outcome was a mixture. Service together, especially danger shared, produces comradeship, which is good for morale and enhances a sense of mutual dependence and collectivity; this sentiment was probably helped out by regional loyalties, where they existed. But, as I recall, the wartime army could not eliminate cynicism about the kind of authority that is based on social rank. That cynicism is a characteristic of industrial society in Britain. It encourages systematic doubt about the worthiness, goodwill, and abilities of those who are in charge, and this disrespect for the managerial or officer class extends to the organization itself, provoking contempt for its paternalistic claims, and resentment of its assumption of effortless superiority over the individual. This sentiment, pushed to its extreme and becoming a true-belief, tells a man that no one in the organization, except he himself and maybe some of his mates, will look after him; it also insists that no one is inherently better than him; it teaches that his real inferiors are those who pretend to be his superiors. That sentiment truly deserves to be called svejkism. I return to this topic later.

DISEDUCATION AND THEATER

Organizations have problems in capitalizing on loyalties already focused elsewhere, because they do not find it easy to make their members *unlearn* the attitudes that they already have. Devotion, in fact, is manufactured in formal organizations by systematic diseducation. This diseducation is partly done by controlling the information that reaches the members, for example by keeping them in a walled community and censoring or otherwise regulating channels of communications. But there are practical limitations, even in the case of prisons, and when the organization has a task to do in the world the regulatory costs can be prohibitive.

The remedy then is to educate members so that they interpret the messages they receive in ways that suit the organization. From a scientific standpoint, one that looks for objective truth, this is diseducation. It produces a style of thinking, and not-thinking, that marks devotion. The trick is done by placing information in a frame that limits the recipient's capacity to think and to doubt. The frames around the stirrup pump, the drill square, the school assembly, the mutual brainwashing about our own excellence that went on at the university, and the other dignity-inducing forms of play, are all of this kind. What they have in common is *poetic performance* or *theater*.

The phrase poetic performance belongs in a family of concepts that includes, among others, ritual, ceremonial, fantasy, play, theater, and rhetoric. These forms of expression are different from one another, but all share the quality of communicating a message that escapes validation by direct measurement against an objective world. Rhetoric should not be contaminated with facts. Verification by an appeal to facts is framed as inappropriate, just as, in the world of science, rhetoric should not be allowed to contaminate factual information.

The word *information* suggests a straightforward, true or false, uncomplicated "bit"-like quality, neutral, uncommitted, scientific, objective, available to anyone who has the technical apparatus to recover it. True information, it seems, is underwritten by an objective reality. So conceived, *information* represents only part of the communication that goes on in any social setting, including formal organizations. Messages are sent with an eye more to their effect than to their truth. Even when the information transmitted takes the *form* of factual stuff, it is often designed to "put a spin" on hard facts. Alternatively, its purpose may be to create "facts" to suit the occasion. This is *rhetoric*, deliberately constructed to persuade and often to mislead. The prime purpose is not to convey information but to create attitudes.

Rhetoric has two forms, one prosaic and the other poetic or theatrical.[19] Persuasion that relies on quasi-logical constructions, that rehearses an argument, that purports to be analytical and reasoned, is ordinary or prosaic rhetoric: persuasion that is simple, assertive, and most of all that goes beyond speech into other kinds of performance constitutes *theater* or *poetics*. The politician who claims to speak for the people and to have their interests at heart, and who talks of his humble home and his honest and industrious parents, is using rhetoric; if the same man presents himself in a cloth cap and uses the unrefined language of the workplace, he is giving a performance. These performances are a de-intellectualized *mindless* kind of rhetoric; one that uses a peculiarly nonrational quality found in poetic "truth."

The "truth" asserted in poetic performances is presented as absolute and unqualified. *Webster's* dictionary describes poetry as "writing that formulates a concentrated imaginative awareness of experience in language chosen and arranged to create a specific emotional response through its meaning, sound and rhythm." Poetry, in other words, affects the emotions more powerfully than does prosaic speech. Poetry lights on feelings, not on consciously analytic capacities. That her dancing is pure poetry is an evaluation offered not as a proposition, backed by evidence and argument, and expecting to be disputed, but as a self-evident and incontestable truth. Poetry's truth is not something that can be measured or experimentally verified. It has

[19]Kenneth Burke, reluctantly separating rhetoric from poetics, suggested that, if there had to be a divergence, it should be in function: poetical expression is intrinsically valued, but rhetoric is always used "for purposes of cooperation and competition" (1966:296). For me, rhetoric and poetics have the same function and are distinguished by form.

the knack of making verification seem inappropriate. Would you want to disconfirm, experimentally, the following?

> My heart is like a singing bird
> Whose nest is in a watered shoot;
> My heart is like an apple-tree
> Whose boughs are bent with thick-set fruit;
> My heart is like a rainbow shell
> That paddles in a halcyon sea;
> My heart is gladder than all these
> Because my love is come to me.

Whatever "truth" those lines possess, it is not captured by a cardiograph. A poem does not invite an empirical verification of what it says, any more than it invites an examination of its logic. Of course there is a whole intellectual industry that examines the structure of poetry (the common meaning of *poetics*), and it may well be that, for those who have the skill, analytic dissection sharpens their enjoyment. But it is not the poetry that they are enjoying. It is another kind of patterning, one that is cool and intellectual and may eventually result in destroying the unschooled enjoyment, when critical analysis reveals flaws in the pattern. Poetry belongs to the body and its rhythms, to the heart, not to the head.[20]

A poetic performance is a profoundly disintellectual thing. It is not an invitation to be rational or analytical, to doubt and to ask questions. It is an enticement directly to feeling and to unquestioning belief; an implantation of values; and in that respect a form of diseducation. It is designed first and foremost not to make people think, but to make them feel. It does so by

[20]Then what of those poets who have an intellectual appeal, like John Donne or Francis Thompson? Do they not demonstrate that poetry can be an intellectual thing, even theological? Indeed they do. But there is still a distinction to be made between the theological or psychological content, which may have its own esthetic appeal, and the enjoyment that can be derived from the music of their words. Read "The Hound of Heaven."

excluding beyond its frame the analytic structuring and calculation that characterizes prosaic everyday life. In particular, of course, the organization's goal—insofar as it is in search of consent and not compliance—is to inhibit the calculation of self-interest, the notion in individual members that they might have an identity which is distinct from and sometimes in competition with the organization which encompasses them.

THE REWARDS OF INCORPORATION

Thus, to the extent that a soldier or a schoolboy is motivated to do his duty by fear of punishment or by hope of reward, the institution has failed to win devotion. It has exacted compliance, but it has not won consent. Dignity should provoke a sense of respect, perhaps awe, but not fear. The institution must have an intrinsic value. Its service is not a job, but a vocation. To ask what one gets in return is to fall from grace, for to ask the question is to deny one's total incorporation in the "body." Dignity, in its least tarnished form, would be achieved by any institution that successfully passed itself off as unambiguously divine; but even the Vatican and the Dalai Lama fall short of that.

But there are spiritual rewards, in a broad sense of the phrase, for the incorporated member. Many of the soldiers I knew enjoyed ceremonial parades. Choral singing in school also gave most of us pleasure, despite the bad-tempered histrionics of the music master and the distress of the headmaster (whose musical sensibilities were visibly bruised by our performances—he would sink his head into his hands). At a somewhat less spiritual level, collectivities of the more collegial kind are given to feasting and celebrating and dressing up. Even organizations that fall at the other end of the spectrum, such as a factory, usually do something about major holidays like Christmas, and the "works outing" (the annual day trip to a resort usually heavily subsidized or even paid for by the firm) was a feature of my childhood. In short, part of an institution's holistic presentation of itself may be the image of a parent and provider; or, to say it less genially, legitimacy and consent can be helped by bread and circuses. "Bread" belongs in the domain of compliance; cheap bread for the Roman mob was a bribe. But the feast that Oxford colleges provide for old members, the gaudy, or the lavish buffet that the new university laid on after the annual graduation ceremony, or the regimental dinners at Christmas when the officers wait on the men, fall into the domain of circus, of consent. They are not material bribes. They are makers of dignity. They belong in a category with other cultural performances that both celebrate and strengthen the joy of surrendering oneself to an institution.

Nevertheless the kind of dignity that is achieved through a quasi-familial image, while it certainly makes for trust and for willing service and a large helping of legitimacy, also contains an element of calculation—a sense that, if I am thrust out of the organization, the important consideration is that it is *I* who will be bereft. There is a covert recognition, both by the institution and its members, of the possibility of a less than fully converted individual, whose service is conditional on suitable reward: not quite the situation of the Australian aborigine at the mission station—"No pray, no tucker!"—but a move in the direction of compliance.

Chapter 3

Dismantling Institutional Dignity

Dulce est desipere in loco.
Playing the fool in the right context is a pleasure.
—Horace

MARKING RANK

Entire and perfect legitimacy is never realized. Some institutions come much nearer to it than others, but perfection always remains a goal and is never an experience. There are individuals who alienate their total identities to an organization, and are ready even to die for it, but no organization seems able to command such devotion from all its members. All of the people get taken in some of the time, Lincoln is supposed to have said, and some of the people all of the time, but not all of the people all of the time.[1] Mystification and the pressure to show devotion seem to be burdensome, and the theater of hierarchy and collectivity provokes either evasion (to be considered later) or a countertheater, which is this chapter's subject.

[1] The saying is attributed also to Lincoln's contemporary, Phineas T. Barnum, better known for "There's a sucker born every minute."

The counterperformance I have in mind is not a direct assault on the institution itself, a simple assertion that the regiment is a "shower" (military slang for an undisciplined rabble), or the school is a dismal washout, or the university a pretentious fake. Nor need it be a direct onslaught on the institution's basic values. The finger seems less often to be pointed at the organization itself than at the people who give the orders and make the decisions. Those who are "of the body" may be devoted to institutional values, even when their day-to-day experience is of being manipulated by those in charge for their own advantage. "The Constitution" and "The American People" (the two ultimate pieties of canting politicians in the United States) are fine; the problem is this or that set of politicians or bureaucrats. Thus institutional dignity can be left intact, while the mockery falls on the agents of efficiency, on their persons and on their offices.[2] Ironically, they are most at risk, even when efficient, if they inflate their images and make too much of their own dignity. Even when the values themselves are denounced (attacks on communism, capitalism, humanism, this or that religion, and so on), persons usually turn out to be handier and more satisfying targets (for love as well as hate) than a disembodied institution, a set of principles, values, and regulations. Emotions demand action and action is most satisfying when the source of evil (or virtue) is concretized in persons. Symbols—burning the flag—are the next best thing, but very disappointing if nobody is seen to get hot under the collar about it.

Institutions, with varying degrees of subtlety, present the drama of themselves at two levels. One is the collectivity, the mystery of the "body": you salute the uniform, not the man. The other level celebrates the owners and masters of the organization, those who wield power. Some leaders apply most of

---

[2]This is a variant of the *principle of adjutancy*. The colonel's infallibility is protected by having an adjutant to take the blame for what goes wrong.

the dignity to *their own persons*, and allow the surplus to trickle down over the organization. In those cases—Hitler, for example—the master himself becomes the body, the breastplate of righteousness, Christlike. At the other extreme, neither of the headmasters who feature in my story could ever have been said to "be" the school; they were too drab. Nevertheless, despite the modesty of the English[3] and their supposed contempt for what in another arena became stigmatized as the "cult of leader-personality," both the school and the university had a set of performances that, by marking inequality, marked not only leadership but also leaders, and at the same time incorporated the institution into those persons, creating a hierarchy.

In charge were the "elders," those near the center of the mystery, the trustees, the holders of tradition, having a power that would supposedly be dangerous in the hands of persons less exalted than themselves. The eminence of these special people was marked by rituals of interaction, as were lesser eminences all the way down the hierarchy. The university went in for this theater of rank least (but it was certainly not absent); the school did it more, and "discipline," which in practice usually meant obedience to the orders of seniors, was an everyday word; and the army wallowed in endless ceremonialized marking of the chain of command.

The point is not simply that seniors gave orders, but that their superiority was indicated by the same kind of mystification that was engineered for the organization itself. Mystification comes easily in a school with its in-built system of age-grades. Boys—I suppose girls too—do this anyway, ranking themselves and being inclined to see mystery and power in those older than them, a year or two being an infinity of time when one is young, and therefore an infinity of accumulated

---

[3]Churchill, the Duke of Wellington, Ernest Bevin, and Mrs. Thatcher all serve as reminders that the myth of the modest, self-effacing Englishman is ironic. It promotes a truth by stating its opposite.

experience. In schools of the kind I attended there is also overt ranking, through the hierarchy of classes, through the offices of form captain and school captain and prefect, and various games captains, and being awarded "colours" for one or another sport; each position marked by the right to command others, by privileges (the prefects had their own common room), by the performance of public rituals that might have other purposes but also signaled the person's status (for example, prefects read the lesson in assembly) and sometimes by distinctive insignia on the clothing.

Universities also go in for visible markers of distinction, but they mark not so much authority as achievement. Doctoral gowns, masters' gowns, bachelors' gowns all indicated one's place in the ladder of attainment; at Oxford even the undergraduates were sorted out, by the length of their gowns, between scholars, exhibitioners, and commoners.[4] The gowns marked a hierarchy; they did not mark a chain of command, and in a rather vague way, all academic members of the university were united as equal servants in the cause of knowledge. But that, so to speak, was the Sunday sermon. The weekday world, at least in some universities, was peopled with master academics and servant academics, rulers and subjects. Ranking was made painfully clear a decade or so after the 1939–45 war, when the academic hierarchy came under attack. Activists, huffing and puffing to blow the old house down, made a somewhat rough adaptation of Marxist ideas about how the state and its associated bureaucracy function during capitalism, and used it to discredit university authorities and to justify their own revolutionary activities. The means of production, which meant the material resources available to the university (buildings, equipment, and money) and its human resources (the labor of students, staff, and faculty), were said to be under the

---

[4]The two former categories held awards given by the college to which they belonged.

control of a ruling "class" consisting of senior faculty and senior administrators. Here is a description of an Australian university.

> There's the professorate. They have their own club that
> doesn't admit even faculty of lower rank; forget about stu-
> dents. Within that group there's a smaller group recruited
> by a system of "interlocking directorships"—the vice-chan-
> cellor, his deputy, the registrar, the chairman of the aca-
> demic board and four or five others. Between them they
> chair every committee that matters in the university. They
> run the place.[5]

Obviously, such people do not in a literal sense own the
institution's property, as mill-owners in nineteenth-century
Britain owned the mills; but they did, like mill-owners then
and managers in industry now, set the conditions of work. In a
manner of speaking, they owned the hierarchy. They also controlled appointments. Like any other ruling class, it was asserted, they used their power to further their own interests,
exploiting the workers, depriving students and junior faculty of
their legitimate right to share control over the means of production: in other words, the "people" did not control the conditions under which they worked and did not enjoy the benefits that their labor created. The "people" were not part of the
institution; they were exploited by those who controlled it.
The revolution, activists said, would put power into the hands
of the "people." In some institutions, usually for a short time,
power did indeed pass from the hands of an old guard to a new
and younger elite. In many places the movement put an end to
the reign of the "God Professor," that autocratic high priest of
academia satirized in the tale of a somewhat inexpert academic

---

[5]Unattributed quotations are taken from interviews conducted in various universities in 1979.

svejk, *Lucky Jim.*[6] Power, of course, did not end up with "the people": it rarely does move far in that direction.

Notice the target. The idea of a university, and in particular its function in the larger community, was much debated. Also, Marxists of one variety or another being in the van of these protests, there was much rhetoric about "the system." But, inevitably when the battle was joined, fire was directed at people, at those who were in charge of the present system and its defence, and there was little Gandhian endeavor to love the people while hating the system they controlled. The system and the institution were concretized into the offices of command and the particular individuals who held those offices.

Svejk's army put the spotlight in the same place; the institution stands second to—or even has its essential existence in—those who lead it. Here is an address by Major Bluher, which eloquently conveys the degree to which power transcends holism in organizations.

> Every officer . . . is, as such, the most perfect being, my men, and has a hundred times more brain than all of you together. You cannot conceive of anything more perfect than an officer, my men, even if you were to think about it all your lives. Every officer is a necessary being, whereas you, my men, are only incidental beings. You may exist but you may not. And if, my men, it came to war and you were to give up your lives for His Imperial Majesty, good, then nothing would change very much. But if, before that, your officer were to fall, then you'd [at once] see how dependent you are on him and what a loss it would be to you. The officer must exist and, in fact, you derive your existence exclusively from the officers; you spring from them. You cannot get on without them. You cannot even fart without your military superiors. For you, my men, an officer is your

[6]This novel, by Kingsley Amis (1954), rode to success on the 1950s wave of disrespect in Britain for all things holistic and hierarchical. See Chapter 6.

moral law whether you understand it or not. (Hasek 1973: 428)

An army celebrates rank every minute of the day and on every inch of its domain. You may salute the uniform and not the man, as we were often told, but that dictum never made us forget that the orders were coming from the man, not from his clothing. Nor did it stop the man with "stripes" (i.e. noncommissioned officers, who were not saluted) becoming godlike, Zeus being the awesome regimental sergeant major (the only NCO who was saluted).

Some level of mystery and remoteness was made to inhere in all but the least of them. The least of them had a bed in one corner of each barrackroom at the training depot. He was called "Trained Soldier" and addressed as such. Those I remember were regular soldiers, unfitted one way or another for more exacting duties.[7] They functioned as tutors and what they taught was the etiquette and ceremony of the barrackroom itself: how to keep that fire hose clean (they were the ones who scrounged and owned—held in trust—the spare fire pump), how to fold blankets properly, how to polish brass, and other useful things like how to report sick, how to darn a sock, and how to fold a sock so that a hole in it would not be visible to the inspecting officer. The trained soldiers came across (to eighteen-year-olds) as tired old men, perhaps even in their thirties, remote, not very approachable, but also not frightening. Their presence was no strain.

That was not so with the drill sergeant, before whom no lesser person dared relax. The barracks were built spider-fashion, the rooms radiating out from a central area which contained the bathrooms and washbasins. Off this central area was a shrine in which lived the drill sergeant in charge of the whole spider. No one went casually to his room; no one ran past it or

---

[7]"Regulars" were those who had enlisted in the peacetime army.

made a noise in its vicinity; the sergeant had his own wash-basin, in line with the rest, but no one else dared use it even when there was a queue for the others. The sergeant did not socialize with those beneath him (sergeants had their own mess) except on rare occasions when he would tell tales about his life in the peacetime army and treat us to regimental lore.

The drill sergeant's primary responsibility was to turn the recruits into not-thinkers, to make them react to commands instantly, without thought and with precision. Not-thinking is, paradoxically, a state of extremely heightened awareness of the presence of a superior person and of the demands he is about to make, and this awareness, felt acutely on parade, was present in every interaction. In fact, being in the vicinity of a superior was to be on parade, and three stripes or, superlatively, a crown on the sleeve, commanded instant attention and a no less instant anxiety that something was about to go wrong. Superiors were a constant source of tension.

> It's an accepted thing that however you answer and what-ever you do a dark cloud will always be hanging over you and the thunder will begin to peal. Without that you can't have discipline. (Hasek 1973: 429)

These particular superiors (noncommissioned officers at the depot) were practiced tension-makers, required to be loudly and continuously abusive, the smallest failing being met with styl-ized ridicule. The schooling in degradation was directed ostensibly at failings in posture or apparel but its ultimate purpose was to habituate a particular kind of response; anger must be controlled and humility shown. Told that one marched like a "pregnant bloody duck" and immediately asked how one marched, one was required to reply in a loud voice, "Like a pregnant bloody duck, Sergeant!"

All in all, one lived a life in the early stages of military train-ing that was emotionally somewhat burdensome, and, perhaps like most campaigns of mystification, this menticidal process seemed to require some dialectical relief, some counterperformance. Relief was obtained through humor.

UNMARKING RANK

Armies like the appearance of order. It is therefore not surprising that symbolic disengagement from military authority can sometimes also be fairly neat and tidy. In fact some of the mockery in armies is licensed or at least partly licensed, and the authorities are able to make good use of disengagement to strengthen their own position. It is also sometimes hard to see much anger underneath the fun of symbolic disengaging. This world is ambiguous, halfway into play, halfway into real protest. If the authorities take offense at what is said or done, one can always plead that "it was all in fun." Indeed, the authorities themselves are expected to play along, to collude in the game.

The abuse that drill sergeants delivered on the barrack square to recruits who had "two left feet" was highly stylized, very rarely personal, and usually touched with the kind of humor that lies in "You got two left feet?" or "Your other left!" screamed at the unfortunate trooper who turns right when ordered to turn left. Anyone whose hair grew beyond the regulation quarter of an inch was not simply told to get a haircut. The drill sergeant stood behind the recruit, breathed down his neck, snorted, and then asked, in an entirely conversational voice, "Does your head hurt, lad?" That required an answer, delivered at maximum volume, "No, sergeant!" The same conversational voice continued, "Well, it ought to, because I'm standing on your hair!" followed by an ear-splitting scream "Get it cut!" Or, when the drills were going particularly badly and everyone in the squad seemed to have two left feet, the following would be delivered with a rising intonation that conveyed contempt mixed with despair, "Household troops? Household troops? If the king saw you, he'd bloody abdicate!"[8]

Abundant abuse is part of the military style in *The Good Soldier Svejk*. Soldiers are routinely addressed as "pigs," "sods," "bastards," "idiots," "scum," and threatened with "a couple across the jaw." It is all part of a philosophy of military education, neatly summarized by Major General von Schwarzburg (Hasek 1973:222):

> A soldier must be kept in a state of terror; he must tremble
> in front of a superior; he must be in mortal dread of him.
> Officers must keep men ten paces from their person and not
> allow them to think independently or even to think at all.

The major general is portrayed as making an idiot of himself. But the drill sergeant, who compared us to "pregnant bloody ducks" and promised us that our deportment would make the monarch abdicate, was doing something different: he was making fun of himself. This is not the plain abuse delivered by Svejk's superiors. Up front, certainly, it is a performance intended to intimidate. But there are messages within messages. Obviously, also, the drill sergeant is not giving a performance that is a simple maker of dignity like the ceremonials described earlier. In his presentation there is an element of self-mockery, and the process of mystification, of making something sacred, is never intendedly ironic. The drill sergeant's humor certainly is stylized and therefore impersonal, but at the same time it announces his humanity, even a simulacrum of individuality: he is not just a drill sergeant, he knows how to stand outside the role and make a joke out of what he has to do.

Humor, in these circumstances, is a breeze that wafts away

[8]Household troops are those nominally employed to guard the sovereign, at that time George VI.

the fumes of devotion-inducing mystification. But it is not a gale; it does no harm to the collectivity, because it is, by definition, not serious. Mockery, in these instances, indicates nothing worse than mild disrespect or perhaps a pretence at disrespect. School life had similar features. Apart from the musical headmaster and his successor, every master had his nickname, mostly simple diminutives of the surname or the first name, sometimes the standard British working class repertoire of "Smudger" for Smith, or "Dusty" for Miller, or "Taffy" for Jones, sometimes more ingenious attributions like "Moby Dick" or "Pimp."[9] Why the headmasters escaped, I do not know. But in the upper sixth we did compose disrespectful comic verses, both in English and in Latin, about one of them, who, when a Latin version fell into his hands, got the situation exactly right by remarking dispassionately that the last line did not scan.

There were also military performances that directly indicated disengagement from the organization and disrespect for its masters. Here is a song (I do not know the tune) from the 1914–18 war.[10]

> We've got a sergeant-major,
> Who's never seen a gun;
> He's mentioned in despatches
> For drinking privates' rum,

[9]A blacksmith's face is smudged and a miller's clothes are dusty. Jones is a Welsh surname and Taffy is an offensive form of a common Welsh Christian name, *Dafydd* (David). *Pimp* is not quite as it sounds. The man was very small and round and we thought "Pimp" to be an abbreviation for "pimple." Maybe some paronomasiac sixth-former, wiser in the ways of the world than the rest of us, had invented the nickname.

[10]Somewhat bowdlerized versions of most of these songs are to be found in Brophy and Partridge 1965. Many of them also appear in the Theatre Workshop play *Oh What a Lovely War*, which is a savage indictment of the British generals who mismanaged the 1914–18 war.

> And when he sees old Jerry
> You should see the bugger run
> Miles and miles and miles behind the lines!

In my memory, that song was no longer in vogue in the 1939–45 war, perhaps because in most campaigns there were no stabilized lines. The same theme, this time with more anger, appears in another 1914–18 song, "The Old Barbed Wire." This tells you where to find various people: the sergeant is drunk on the canteen floor, the quartermaster is miles and miles and miles behind the line, the C.O. is skulking in the deepest dugout, the sergeant major is "boozing up the privates' rum," but the battalion (that is, the ordinary soldier) is "hanging [dead] on the old barbed wire."

Paradise was an amiable fantasy of an inverted hierarchy, which recalls peasant fantasies of a world turned upside down, the hare chasing the hounds, and the donkey riding on its master's back.[11] The soldiers' imagining was less bucolic, as in this song (sung to the tune of "What a Friend We Have in Jesus"):

> When this sodding war is over,
> O, how happy we will be!
> NCOs will all be navvies,
> Privates ride in motor cars.
> NCOs will smoke their Woodbines,
> Privates puff their big cigars.[12]

There were also chants, like the following far from amiable "Greeting to the Sergeant":

> You've got a kind face, you old bastard,
> You ought to be bloodywell shot:

[11]Burke 1978: 185–91.

[12]A navvy is a manual laborer. The word is an ironical abbreviation of "navigator." Navvies dug canals which facilitated inland navigation. Woodbine (a trade name) was a small cheap cigarette.

You ought to be tied to a gun-wheel,
And left there to bloodywell rot.

There were recitations, imported into the army from the "working class," according to Brophy and Partridge (1965:64), that rejoiced in defiance by the weak. This one was still going strong in the 1939–45 war.

It was Christmas Day in the workhouse,
The season of good cheer.
The paupers' hearts were merry,
Their bellies full of beer.
In came the workhouse master,
And strode about the halls,
And wished them Merry Christmas,
But the paupers answered "Balls!"
This peeved the workhouse master,
And he swore by all the gods
"There'll be no Christmas pudding
For you dirty rotten sods."
Then up spoke one old pauper,
With a voice as bold as brass
"You can take your Christmas pudding,
And stick it up your arse."

Some other songs, which I remember surviving into the 1939–45 war, indicated not so much defiance as resignation, boredom, frustration, a lack of enthusiasm and a sense of being a nothing, an instrument of another's purposes. The following was sung to the tune of "Auld Lang Syne": "We're 'ere, because we're 'ere, because we're 'ere, because we're 'ere, because . . ."

There were other songs, many of them vulgar, that reek of disengagement. The following, which parodied a popular ballad from the 1914 music halls ("On Sunday I Walk Out with a Soldier"), was still helping in the next war to make route marches less disagreeable:

> I don't want to join the army,
> I don't want to go to war.
> I'd rather hang around Piccadilly Underground,
> Living off the earnings of a high-born lady.
> Don't want a bayonet up my arse-hole,
> Don't want my bollocks shot away.
> I'd rather stay in England,
> Merry, merry England,
> And fornicate my bleeding life away.

Evidently a better way to die than hanging on the old barbed wire.

A few songs abandoned not only the collectivity but even comradeship, and are the ultimate expression of individuality (and resignation). The following was a parody of a Salvation Army song; it addresses fallen comrades.

> The bells of hell go ting-a-ling-a-ling
> For you but not for me.
> The devils how they sing-a-ling-a-ling
> For you but not for me.
> O Death, where is thy sting-a-ling-ling,
> O grave thy victory?

Such songs probably do not add to the dignity of the army, and the philosophy of life they celebrate is the very reverse of devotion to a collectivity. But "disengagement" songs are not necessarily unambivalent indicators of disaffection. The savage irony, found especially in 1914–18 songs, certainly suggests this. But satire of this kind has a strange capacity to strengthen an organization, while simultaneously denigrating it. Paradoxically, the songs raise morale by lightening the burden of mystification, in just the same way as do nicknames, or sergeants who display a stylized sense of humor. They diminish disaffecting tendencies merely by venting them. Indeed, some symbolic forms of nonconsent—for example, rites of reversal, like the army custom of having the officers wait on the men at

Christmas dinner—are accepted by organizations as proper, in spite of the way they invert the official hierarchy.

The mockery and the irony point away from the collectivity as a mystical and indivisible entity, and toward the individuals who make it up, and in particular toward the fact of inequality. The sergeant diminishes himself and his remoteness, by self-mockery. At Christmastime the officer plays a one-meal carnival and puts on the mask of a servant. Those down below do not make fun so much of the school or the regiment (this does happen sometimes) but of those who are in charge of the organization, those who are seen as its owners, sometimes as individuals (for example, nicknames), sometimes as a class (when roles are reversed, or in a thoroughly suggestive 1914–18 song about staff officers playing leap frog and jumping over each other's backs).

These performances indicate that the members have not been absorbed entirely into the body of the organization; they do not see it only as a collectivity. Beneath the official ideology that follows St. Augustine, proclaiming there is no salvation outside the institution, there is a submerged ideology that denies and mocks the official claims.[13] In this way every organization is made to recognize its own incapacity to make hierarchy prevail entirely. Every organization has some measure of latent alienation, of disaffection that is recognized and tacitly permitted in ironic performance or in direct satire.

The ironic performances and the satirical songs and chants are not direct threats against the organization. The ironic performance in particular is offered as a joke, something that need not be taken seriously; which is, of course, a neat piece of mystification. Do not take seriously the fact that we behave as if we do not take the organization seriously! The sergeant's jokes are stylized jokes, and therefore official. Military carnival is controlled; when the officers wait on the men, the sergeant

---

[13] *Salus extra ecclesiam non est.*

major is in attendance to make sure that nobody "takes a liberty."

Sometimes an organization may go on the offensive and itself stage a performance that mocks individualism. In 1971 an engagingly Pollyanna-ish book was published with the title *The Administrative Revolution: Notes on the Passing of Organization Man.* It trumpeted the ideas of a "lanky, amiable, pipe-smoking professor from the Midwest," who advocated putting "self-direction" in place of authoritarian management and the insistence on conformity (Berkley 1971:15). Self-direction can take many forms, one of which is "the current attempt to see the group as a creative vehicle" (Whyte 1957:57–59). A collective search for a new idea, in its extreme form, is called "brainstorming," and is performed by what would otherwise be considered a committee. But it is less a committee than an undisciplined rabble of individuals, everyone firing off ideas without much regard for what others have said, shouting, interrupting, going off at a tangent, in happy disregard of rank and status and the customary etiquette of intellectual exchange. In fact such antics minister less to the intellect than to the emotions, relaxing the tensions that go with holism and hierarchy. If any idea emerges as a consensus when the intoxication passes, it usually is something that was around already.

This performance inverts bureaucratic normality, and in an ironic way recognizes the perils of training members to not-think. It takes on the mantle of efficiency, but in fact it is a form of theater, a way of disclaiming an identity by making fun of it. A performance of this kind quite deliberately lays aside organizational dignity and celebrates individualism. But it is still mostly a performance, resembling the ritual inversions of army life. It is a pretense that the hierarchy leaves room for individualism. It is also, given the extremes of silliness to which brainstormers may go, a form of irony; a performative mockery of individualism. It is obviously not the real thing, because the indiscipline of brainstorming is strictly limited to the occasion. The organization man who indulges in such behavior whenever he feels the urge will find himself in trouble.

Organizations inherit, so to speak, from the larger society in which they exist, in particular from societies of the past when the ranking system was less ambiguous than it has become in modern industrial society, a tradition of puncturing overinflated authority. Peasants created theatrical and satirical representations of themselves, their masters, and their society. There is an extensive literature on disengagement in peasant societies, rich enough to reveal complexities that are not visible in the military satire described above.

The literature has its beginnings in the nineteenth-century work of folklorists, most of whom were uninterested in questions of power. Their successors, beginning about thirty years ago, have shifted the center of attention to the politics of cultural performances, a favored one being carnival. The word *carnival* is a rendering into English of a Latin phrase which means "goodbye meat," and it refers to several days of merrymaking that take place before Lent, the period between Ash Wednesday and Easter spent by good Christians in penitence and fasting to mark Christ's time in the wilderness. Carnival anticipates Lent by reversing it; it is a time for gaiety and feasting and dancing and going to the fair to have a good time. It is also a time for excesses: for eating too much, and drinking too much, and wenching and fornicating. Revelers may wear masks and so put aside their everyday identities. At carnival time one can do in the open what at other times should not be done at all, or should at least be done discreetly. It is a time, in other words, for reversing not simply the austerities of Lent but also the conventions of normal everyday life. The conventions are Rousseau's chains, now temporarily removed. Included in this overturning of normal etiquette and modesty are the conventions that give the mighty and the humble their separate identities. People go about the streets acting the fool and playing practical jokes on one another, and, everyone being equal in the anonymity of the carnival mask, anyone can be a victim.

Tomfoolery is not confined to carnival. In Britain annual fairs were held on the days of certain saints, for example St. Martin (he was the patron of drunkards), St. Giles, St. Michael, and St. Bartholemew, and they were occasions for just the kind of free expression that I have described for carnival; so much so that St. Bartholemew's fair in London, founded in 1133, was closed by disapproving Victorians in 1855. Nor is the flouting of authority and propriety found only among Christians. Hindu women are expected in public to be models of decorum, self-effacing before men. But during the festival of Holi gangs of young women shed their modesty and roam the streets armed with brass syringes filled with dye, which they squirt over any man they encounter (or woman, if important enough). Young persons, boys and girls, normally in India expected to be deferential, are similarly armed and ready to attack their elders.

These occasions are not riots nor are they supposed to be opportunities for criminal acts, although they sometimes turned that way—that was the reason given for closing St. Bartholemew's fair in nineteenth-century England. The horseplay and the disrespect were licensed by the authorities. Kings had their fools and jesters, whose only task was to mock authority. Kings and other dignitaries, such as the lord mayor of London, appointed a Lord of Misrule (in Scotland called the Abbot of Unreason) to organize silliness. In my childhood students at the local university held a "Rag Day" in aid of local hospitals: processions, fancy dress, boisterous disruption of public occasions, a kind of comprehensive trick-or-treat in which shopkeepers and civic dignitaries were required to ransom immunity by making a contribution to charity.

Organized silliness is like planned spontaneity, an oxymoron that neatly catches the contradiction between order and disorder that pervades the entire domain. Lords should not, if things are normal, be associated with misrule; normal abbots are wise and reasonable men, and fools should not become abbots. There is a complicated play of ideas in the titles and in the customs. Peasant villages in Europe allowed the equivalent of a year-round carnival for young men, who were licensed to play the fool.[14] They were called Companies of Fools in northern Italy, or Silly Ones (*Stolti*) or Donkeys (*Asini*) or Madmen (*Pazzi*). In France they were called *Fous*, the Fools or the Innocent Ones. *Madmen* or *donkeys* suggests creatures which are partly but not entirely outside the boundaries of normal civilized human interaction, because they cannot be relied upon to respond in normal ways. *Fool*, or more particularly *innocent*, shifts the image: the innocent person is one who is without guilt, one who has not been corrupted, one who is therefore good, without guile. In this sense children are innocent, unaware of evil. But at the same time they are unaware of duty, and therefore they stand outside society. The suggestion is of a condition of purity, which is achieved at the other end of life by redemption, being freed from earthly obligations. The innocent, in short, are those who have not been corrupted by conventions, particularly because they do not experience, still less exercise, authority.

Seen in those terms the follies of carnival and fairs and of the Companies of Fools are the very epitome, the perfectly comprehensive miniature, of disengagement (in its symbolic form) from authority. Everything is represented: the state of innocence and purity, which is equivalent to *non*rule; corruption which is *mis*rule; the innocent given the titles of rulers (lords and abbots) and then conducting themselves like donkeys, so that the quality of innocence is shifted into the domain of rational judgment and thus becomes stupidity; inversions and ambiguities and ambivalences and multivocality and ludic

[14]See Milano 1925.

performance enough to satisfy the hungriest postmodernist scholar.

On a less abstracted level the Lord of Misrule, the Abbot of Unreason, their followers, and the Companies of Fools are a straightforward mockery of civil and ecclesiastical authorities. We *play* the fool; but our masters *are* fools. That is the message. But if that is the message, why did authorities allow it to be sent? They did not always, and when they decided things were getting out of hand, they closed down the fairs or took action against the excesses of *I Stolti*. Nevertheless organized tomfoolery was a legitimate part of peasant society, and still is in modern society and in formal organizations, anywhere where authority is exercised.

There are two linked questions. First, why did the common people behave in that way? Second, why did the authorities permit it? A standard functional explanation is that people do not know what is right and good until they have experienced what is wrong and bad. It is said that law is best known in the breach, meaning that one is made most aware of what a law or a custom is when one sees those who break it punished. As a statement of *consequence*—what happens when a law is broken and what one learns from the official reaction—this is indisputable. But it does not explain why people indulge in carnival and enjoy the folly, for they surely do not consciously play the fool to remind themselves what wisdom is. It might explain why artful authorities put up with it; so that they have a chance to "make an example" of an offender. But the notion does not address the question of *motivation* for tomfoolery.

Motivation is addressed by a commonsense metaphor about safety valves. The build-up of resentment occasioned by authority is released in play, in a manner that is relatively harmless: it does not fundamentally weaken the power of those who dominate. On the contrary, it may serve to strengthen that power by lowering the resentment of those who are oppressed and exploited. The weak are deluded into imagining, at least for a time, that their misery is not the reality, that the masters cannot everywhere and always hold them in chains. This is, as I said, a commonsense theory, epitomized in the phrase *letting off steam*. Again, it is indisputable; this really is the sensation people get from all kinds of play, including playing the fool.

It is sometimes argued, however, that motivation, even if correctly identified, is not what makes organized folly significant. Folly matters because it is both an image of resistance to authority and an evolutionary step toward practical resistance and eventually organized protest. Mockery is a move towards defiance, and defiance leads to revolt. Mockery is a way of making a statement about oppression, and a way to raise political consciousness. At the very least, mockery is a rejection of the hegemonic myth put about by the ruling class to boost its own legitimacy. What merit is there in this argument, which sees in the excesses of carnival behavior an articulation and therefore strengthening of resentment?

First, it seems to directly contradict the safety valve theory, because it implies that symbolic theatrical disengagement helps build up the head of revolutionary steam. But in practice there is no necessary contradiction. Nothing is always and perfectly of a piece; things vary from one place to another, from one occasion to another, from one person to another. Messages sent out are differently interpreted by different people. It *may* indeed have been the case that those engaged ostensibly in tomfoolery saw themselves as protesting a system and making themselves ready for the more practical challenge of rebellion or revolution. Purple hair and other skinhead fashions *may* be a protest against industrial capitalism. Certainly authorities often behave as if they were, and take alarm at what they consider to be distasteful or threatening ways of playing the fool. But it is not always so; there may be no threat intended. To deny this possibility is to ignore the huge element of plain enjoyment that is conspicuous in fairs and carnivals; more people are playing the fool for the fun of it than with the conscious aim of subverting a regime, and a hangover is more often the outcome of carnival than is a revolution.

Moreover, if one looks more closely at what the Companies of Fools did, it becomes more difficult to see them as embryonic revolutionaries. The butt of *I Stolti* was not always the ruling class, the gentry and the clergy and the avaricious merchant. If an old man married a young woman, or, worse, if an older woman married a young man, they were treated to *charivari*, in English called "rough music," serenaded on their wedding night with the beating of pans and trays and a cacophonous ribaldry, and sometimes finding the threshold of their house barricaded with cowmuck. There was a vast array of potential victims: a jilted girl; a girl marrying out of the community; the village priest if there were no marriages during carnival; a cuckold; the henpecked husband; and many others who in some way, often inadvertently, offended the norms of peasant life. It is as if beneath the grand protective panoply of state law that brings order to peasant life, there is a space and a need for the sanctioning of trivia, of little conventions that give peasants their identity and make them what they are by instructing them how to behave. The state—the lords and the gentry and the bishops—mostly ignore such matters, just because they are not affairs of state. Leaders do not have to know everything about their subjects' lives, only what will serve to maintain dominance. It may even be that leaving this regulatory space to be occupied by the ordinary people helps perpetuate their illusion that they have freedom, so making them more tractable. Certainly it is hard to find a consciousness of deprivation and the seeds of political awareness and revolution in the indignities that peasants heaped on one another, under the guise of playing the fool, so as to protect the conventions of peasant society. From this point of view, the reality is not revolution but, again, the safety valve.[15]

---

[15]It is also the *principle of the fish*. The great ones eat small ones, that need yet smaller ones to feed upon.

There is no single answer to the question that asks what carnival and other kinds of licensed folly or licensed symbolic disengagement signified. The performances were presentations that sent out different messages on different occasion, and different messages to different people on the same occasion. All that one should do is look closely at the particular instances and see who sent the message and guess what their intentions were, and then look at who received the message and how they behaved when they received it, and then use that behavior to determine the significance of the message. Such tests will reveal occasions that are revolutionary and others that are merely letting off steam; they will also often show that the sender's expectation did not coincide with the receiver's interpretation.

The hierarchy of a peasant society is relatively simple, and makes for distance and separation between the peasants and their masters. The hierarchy of an industrial society also sets masters and subjects as antagonists, but at the same time makes them mutually dependent and keeps them constantly interacting. The effect is to make organized practical protest possible in industrial societies; and organized protest, to the extent that it succeeds, makes theatrical disengagement redundant. Workers, it seems, are better equipped for reality testing than are peasants; they better understand how the hierarchy works and how it may be contested. The context of an industrial society disinvites *fantasies* of disengagement and invites its *practice*. I will have more to say on practice later.

But nothing is ever all of a piece, and theatrical disengagement does occur in modern industrial society, not, as with the peasants, throughout an entire class but in certain marginalized groups or categories, some of which spread across class boundaries. This is the theater of gays and lesbians, of the various forms of black protest in the United States, of the London Carnival organized by West Indians, and of various other manifestations of what now is called popular culture.

The study of popular culture, when it began, was less narrowly focused. In 1958, Richard Hoggart wrote a book about working-class culture in Britain. In that work the concept *culture* was used in a hybrid fashion that combined the anthropological use (beliefs and values, an entire way of life) with the more restricted everyday use that refers to style and fashion and performance and composition and the arts generally. The movement began as an attempt to do for the industrial working class what folklorists and others in earlier generations had done for rural folk: capture a style of life and its unique forms before everything vanished under the homogenizing influence of modernity.

Twenty years later the study of popular culture was on a different tack. Popular culture became the culture of protest. It was no longer the culture of the working class at large but of those (mostly within that class) who were particularly alienated, and who found an important part of their identity in resistance to authority. This identity pertains not to particular individuals, but to categories that in one or another way are marginalized. For example, some working-class schoolchildren refuse to acquire the bourgeois skills that the school system offers them, and thus remain on society's lower edge.[16] These and similar identities are founded on a sentiment of alienation, of disillusion, of wanting no place in the conventional scheme of things, and of having no hope of changing that scheme. These are the cultures of minorities, of people who refuse to be socialized into the conventions that the majority seek to impose.[17]

Reversing the concerns of anthropologists who took their lead from Robert Redfield,[18] scholars of popular culture are not much interested in charting the difference between high and

[16]See Willis 1981.

[17]A strikingly empathetic analysis of a counterculture appears in Berger 1981.

[18]See Redfield 1956.

low culture nor in showing how the high might give shape to the low (other than by providing the negative image). Instead, having demonstrated that the prevailing culture fails to be communicated to particular marginalized segments of the population, they seek to uncover the political significance of popular culture. The songs that people sing, the music that they like, the performances they put on, the clothes that they wear and their cosmetic styles, the way they choose to spend their leisure, their very deportment, all signify not just their difference from the ruling classes and what Redfield would have called the *great tradition*, but also and more significantly their disengagement from it and its bourgeois philosophy.

These disengagers resemble the peasant who gives the finger to the gentry through satirical performances and fantasies of the world upside down. There is an element of carnival in what they do: a rejection of conventional proprieties and values. Also, as with peasant performances, much of it is pure fun, the carefree shedding of responsibility displayed in the various kinds of peasant horseplay. But it is not all fun. There is a variety of modern popular cultural performance that bears a curious resemblance to the quite nastily victimizing and convention-upholding activities of the Companies of Fools. This is the culture of the skinheads, neofascist groups of young people, mostly male, who terrorize those who break social conventions by what they do (in particular homosexual males and the category called "punk") or by what they are (blacks, Pakistanis, Indians, Vietnamese). Skinheads think of themselves as the prime upholders of the fundamental values of their society, which they define as manliness, direct action, patriotism, racial purity, and the like.

The present-day hippielike disengagers and the more sinister skinhead bullies have a straight ancestry back through industrial working-class life to the tolerated or licensed forms of youthful disorder found in peasant societies. To some small extent they constitute a protest, symbolic or practical, against authority. But they are motivated, one suspects, much less by ideas of redistributing power than by the sheer pleasure that they get from expressing themselves, by what they consider fun. That word is often used to describe plain brutality; Paki-bashing, gang rapes, or mayhem on the football terraces are said to be ways of "having fun." Such excesses are part of a long human tradition in which the weak take out their frustrations on the weaker. Nor would I classify what they do as "dismantling dignity." There is no element of satire aimed at those in authority—at least no conscious element (there is surely an irony in the spectacle of a shaven-headed bully in boots and braces representing himself as the ultimate guardian of ruling-class virtues). There is no genuine play and what they call "fun" is seriously criminal. Dignity, it seems, can be dismantled to the point where savagery takes over.

FLANNELING AS A CULTURAL PERFORMANCE

I now return to the army and to a mode of action which, when compared to that of skinheads, is the very model of subtlety and sophistication.

There were some soldiers who either could not or would not cope with the finicking minutiae of military life, and were constantly in one or another kind of minor trouble with the NCOs and the officers for being "idle" (other soldiers called them "awkward"). They were not admired by their comrades, who for the most part pitied them, but mixed with the pity a greater or lesser degree of contempt. At best they were considered unfortunate, hapless, but they were rarely seen as victims of the system, and certainly they were not symbols of resistance to authority, because true defiance is not inadvertent.

There were other soldiers who were deliberately defiant, but in such a way as to avoid trouble. Their performances did symbolize disengagement, and in a fashion different from licensed mockery, because they went beyond what the organization permitted and conducted themselves in a manner that the organization would have liked to prevent. Official inadequacy, on these occasions, signals the limitations of organizational theater, of ceremonially induced devotion. One such performance was flanneling.

Flanneling is a subtly ironic variant of *scrimshanking*, which, the *Concise Oxford Dictionary* says, is "military slang" and is to "shirk duty." *Scrimshanking* was in fashion in the first world war and earlier, and by the 1939–45 war the word had become somewhat archaic. Neither the *Concise Oxford* nor *Webster's* dictionary gives a derivation, but I will invent one to suit my argument: the noun *scrim* is the loosely woven fabric that can be dyed brown and green to make a camouflage net, thus indicating that the truth of what one is doing is not out in the open, and that beneath appearances there is a different reality.

The dictionary definition fails to suggest the concept's richness: there are many ways of shirking duty. The range includes, among other skills, "dodging" or "dodging the column," which Brophy and Partridge (1965:111) describe as "the art and science of avoiding unpleasant and especially dangerous duties"; "swinging the lead,"[19] which is lying to authorities, especially feigning illness (also called "malingering"); "having it cushy," as in "a cushy billet," meaning an unearned freedom from onerous duties or conditions (from the Hindustani word for happiness); "wangle," "scrounge," "win" (suggesting a lottery) or "liberate," all of them ways of obtaining something to which one is not, by the rules of the organization, entitled; and many others.

The verb *shirk* carries the suggestion of being mean and self-

---

[19] Swinging the lead, boys,
Swinging the lead.
Always remember
To work your head.
     Words to go with the bugle call "Pay Parade."

ish. In fact the negative connotations come mostly from authorities, as I mentioned earlier, and ordinary Joes and Jills of my acquaintance, whether or not they are scrimshankers, more often are mildly approving than disapproving, or sometimes envious, of those who bamboozle their superiors. It depends, of course, on whose ox is being gored. If the losers are officials, ordinary Joe will usually applaud. Thus the moral verdict (on whether or not scrimshanking is wicked) is relative, a matter of opinion. Its legal status, on the other hand, since the institution is the lawgiver, is quite unambiguous; scrimshanking, in any form, is an offence.

Scrimshanking is a performance by which scrimshankers tell themselves and the world what they are, how they define themselves. But that raises a question about audiences. The theater of leadership poses no problem. Leaders make themselves visible by presenting a persona, an image or a mask; and their effectiveness in some measure depends on other people having a clear idea of who they are, what they are doing, why they are doing it, and what they stand for. (What they are really doing may well be quite otherwise—Watergate and Irangate and the like; but such things are not advertised and therefore are not, until disclosed, within the domain of theater.)

Neither is what the scrimshanker does openly advertised. The scrimshanker who proclaims to all and sundry that he has dodged the column is likely to find himself sent under escort to join it, or certainly marked down for a dangerous position in the next column. To let it be known that a possession was "liberated" is to invite its confiscation and a charge of theft. In other words, scrimshanking must always be covert. Unlike leaders, scrimshankers keep a low profile. If that is so, how can there be a theater of scrimshanking?

There are two answers. The simple one, which is half the truth, is that there are two potential audiences: authorities who are not admitted, and the scrimshanker's peers, who are invited to admire the theatrical performances celebrating the shirker and his negative (as the authorities see them) achievements. Some forms of scrimshanking are open only to one's peers: scrounging and wangling and dodging the column.[20] But flanneling is more subtle, being so framed that the authorities are an audience, but cannot acknowledge, without confounding themselves, that they have seen the performance. Flanneling masks itself behind a false openness, which, in the manner of an open secret, allows itself to be known, but not to be openly acknowledged.

How is flanneling done, and what does it signify? The word does not appear in Brophy and Partridge's little glossary of military slang. My recollection of its general meaning is this: to pay excessive compliments is to flannel someone, the purpose being manipulation, and such behavior could be rejected by an adjectival modifier, as in the comment "That's just dirty flannel!" In the context of military etiquette the word referred to an extravagant performance of rituals of deference, or the ostentatious display of attitudes and emotions that commend themselves to authorities.[21]

On the surface this assiduity looks like apple polishing or bootlicking. But they are not the same. Apple polishing is unambiguous and unsubtle: it means sedulous and conspicuous adherence to the norms of the organization so as to gain the favor of authorities and thus advance oneself. That final phrase is the differentiator: flannelers are not out to advance them-

---

[20]That proposition, *mutatis mutandis*, is also true of a leader. Cronies may be privy to a theatrical performance marking an identity that is very different from the public image presented to the world at large.

[21]Flannel is a woolen cloth, woven smooth and without nap. The slang term may pick up the idea of warmth and comfort, conveyed by swaddling the target in layers of institutional values. The *Random House Dictionary* gives the verb two meanings: to speak with a thick accent; and to speak smoothly and deceptively. The latter approximates my meaning.

selves within the organization, but rather to distance themselves from it. They do so because in flanneling the elaborate display of deference or of enthusiasm signals just the opposite.

A prominent figure in the scrimshankers' hall of fame is Good Soldier Svejk. Here is an account of Svejk being put through the mill by a panel of army doctors, determined to prove that he is a malingerer and that he is fit for military service, despite the fact that he "had left military service years before, after having been finally certified by an army medical board as an imbecile" (Hasek 1973:3). On this renewed encounter with the military he had already experienced, along with other malingerers, several days of being fed aspirin to induce sweating, and quinine to offend his palate. His stomach had been pumped out twice a day and he had been given enemas with glycerine and soap, and wrapped in a sheet soaked in cold water. Those were the army's standard cures for malingering.

> "It'll be a bloody miracle," roared the chairman [of the panel] at Svejk, "if we don't get the better of you."
>
> Svejk looked at the whole commission with the godlike composure of an innocent child.
>
> The senior staff doctor came up close to Svejk:
>
> "I'd like to know, you swine, what you're thinking about now."
>
> "Humbly report, sir, I don't think at all."
>
> "Himmeldonnerwetter," bawled one of the members of the commission, rattling his sabre. "So he doesn't think at all. Why in God's name don't you think, you Siamese elephant?"
>
> "Humbly report, I don't think because that's forbidden to soldiers on duty. When I was in the 91st regiment some years ago our captain always used to say 'A soldier mustn't think for himself. His superiors do it for him. As soon as a soldier begins to think he's no longer a soldier, but a dirty, lousy civilian. Thinking doesn't get you anywhere. . . . '"
>
> [Then the chairman loses his temper.] "Shut your mug!

We know all about you. . . . You're cunning, you're foxy, you're a scoundrel, you're a hooligan, you're a lousy bastard, do you understand . . .?"

"Humbly report, sir, I understand."

"I've already told you to shut your mug. Did you hear?"

"Humbly report, sir, I heard that I must shut my mug."

"Himmelherrgott, then shut it! When I give you orders, you know very well you must stop talking rot!"

"Humbly report, sir, I know well I must stop talking rot."
(Hasek 1973:76)

This is caricature, the subtleties of real flanneling removed, so that the author can make absolutely clear on which side the imbecility really lies. Svejk is, predictably, sent off to the garrison jail, so that the jailers can "knock all this drivel out of his head." But the incident, crude though it is (and despite the dated schoolboy vocabulary used by the translator), will make clear the peculiar finesse that flanneling requires.

The essence of flanneling is a performance that uses the forms of respect to show disrespect, and in such a way that the target (in this case the officer) will be contradicting himself if he takes offense, and so will be made to look foolish. He cannot, within the frame of military values, object to being shown respect, and he has no simple way of proving that these are just the forms of respect, and not the real thing. That is the point of the reiterated "Humbly report, sir" followed by an exact verbal acceptance of the order given, the acknowledgment itself being an act of disobedience; but invited, indeed made inevitable, by the officer's preceding question:

"I've already told you to shut your mug. Did you hear?"
"Humbly report, sir, I heard that I must shut my mug."

That is the quintessence of flanneling and of certain other forms of scrimshanking: using the proclaimed values of the organization to defeat those values.

The Svejk vignette suggests another form of scrimshanking: malingering. To malinger is to feign illness in order to avoid duty. Svejk's comrades had a well-stocked folk pharmacopeia for inducing the symptoms of strokes, fever, dislocated joints, and worse afflictions—most of them, including, apparently, genuine illness, swiftly remedied by the enema treatment, the stomach pump, and the regime of wet sheets. Bodily ailments are straightforward statements; a simple invocation of the army's rule that soldiers must be physically fit. Malingering is then a rather direct misuse of a military value, physical fitness, to avoid duty. Svejk's affliction is being an imbecile. That too, at first sight, is relatively straightforward: soldiers must carry out orders and genuine half-wits will not understand an order.

But Svejk's manner of demonstrating his imbecility is not at all straightforward. He does not take off his clothes, or babble about rosemary for remembrance and pansies for thoughts, or needing a south wind before he can tell a hawk from a hand-saw. All he does is say "Humbly report, sir" and assert, time and again, an apparently unswerving and unthinking allegiance to military values and the military way of life; that, it seems, together with the "godlike composure of an innocent child," is construed as faking idiocy. Why, one may ask, should such behavior constitute a plausible (if, in Svejk's present case, ineffective) claim to imbecility?

There is a similar scene earlier in the book. Svejk is arrested in a pub by a plainclothes policeman, an *agent provocateur*, for speaking "high treason." Eventually he is taken before a panel of psychiatrists, who deliver the following report:

> The undersigned medical experts certify the complete mental feebleness and congenital idiocy of Josef Svejk, who appeared before the aforesaid commission and expressed himself in terms such as: 'Long live our Emperor Franz Joseph I', which utterance is sufficient to illuminate the state of mind of Josef Svejk as that of a patent imbecile. (1973:30)

The author of the novel, like Svejk, was a Czech, and the sentiment sounds like robust satire: any Czech who wishes long life to the Austrian emperor has to be crazy. But, as you will see, Svejk's imbecility has a set of meanings that are more convoluted than that.

Meanwhile, what is it that converts the show of deference into disrespect? Flanneling is, of course, a form of irony, which is saying one thing, while conveying its opposite, and inviting the collusive understanding of an audience. The Greek word *eiron* means a dissembler. Socratic irony is a pretence of ignorance designed to trap or provoke an antagonist in argument. Irony is also saying one thing, while conveying its opposite, and compelling the reluctant collusion of the victim. All these functions—dissembling, pretending ignorance, provoking an opponent, presenting appearances which are not the reality—neatly fit Svejk's flanneling. Irony inheres in the conjunction of "Humbly report, sir" with words that instantly disobey the order received, by the very act of obeying it; it constitutes mockery.

Irony is simple enough to understand, but to give a name to the trope is not to explain why it is effective. To do that, one must set the use of irony in the context not only of interactions between Svejk, his comrades and his hapless persecutors, but also of the institution in which they all served. The feature that makes flanneling possible is an overabundance of institutional theater. Like every institution, an army has two faces, one prosaic and the other theatrical; one instrumental and the other expressive; one to do with efficiency and the other with dignity; one corresponding roughly to Max Weber's world of the legal-rational, and the other to his world of magic and enchantment.

The instrumental (efficiency) side of a military institution is in principle simple to understand. An army is rationally designed to carry out certain tasks for which force may be required. It operates in a hard world, in which truth lies somewhere between the referential (the truth of a proposition is validated by its correspondence to something out there in the real world—pull out this pin and release the lever and the grenade will explode) and the pragmatic (truth is whatever does us good to believe is true—for example, that God is on our side or that we are formidable).[22] It is a mostly positivist, would-be scientific world; an empirical world that deals in hard testable propositions, which, if they are hard enough to survive the testing, or if they are certified by a recognized authority, become facts.[23]

The other side of military life is the systematic and sustained attempt, described earlier, to routinize enchantment. That sounds like an oxymoron and a situation that will cancel itself—unrelenting enchantment should end up in disenchantment; but in fact the process is, within limits, not immediately self-defeating. The newly recruited civilian is transformed from a calculating self-concerned individual into, as the captain in Svejk's regiment explained, a not-thinker; a perfected automaton who has no identity outside the army's nesting collectivities. The well-trained soldier no longer has—at least is no longer supposed to have—an effective individual identity. He is, in a quite literal sense, uniformed. The army aims to have no shirkers, for shirking is the practical application of individuality. The army leaves no room, at least front-stage, for the

[22]Regimental mottos are often of that kind. The motto of Scottish regiments is *Nemo me impune lacessit* (No one provokes me with impunity). *Poilu*, the generic nickname for a French soldier, means "mettlesome" or "courageous" (literally, "hairy").

[23]In armies, as in any bureaucracy, once such facts are established and certified, they tend to become *super*facts: gospel truth, never again to be questioned, truth-by-convention rather than truth-by-correspondence. (Scrimshankers, in their own indirect way, do question such "facts," and that is why scrimshanking can be useful; it reintroduces reality.)

theatrical expression of individuality. Official military theater celebrates only values that uphold the collectivity.

In practice, as noted earlier, individual identities are rarely totally suppressed. Individuals, either severally or collectively, reject the organization's demands for total loyalty and continue serving their own ends or the ends of some other organization. The rejection may take four forms. One, not considered in this book, is open protest (through mutiny or strikes or counter-organization, for example in trade unions). The second is evasion (concealing noncompliance), the subject of the next chapter. The third is licensed mockery, and the fourth is the irony of Svejk's "Humbly report, sir." These four forms of defiance each use different kinds of theater.

A poetic performance of frank defiance—raising the red flag, being openly insolent to a superior, sit-ins, strikes, teach-ins, and the like—has two features that do not recommend it to a svejk. First, it may decisively shift the interaction out of the theatrical arena into the routinized compound of Weber's iron cage, in a rather literal sense: Svejk goes to the garrison jail to have "all this drivel knocked out of his head." Second, in the symbolic world, it does not necessarily assert the svejk's *individual* identity, but only proclaims devotion to other gods, as the example of the red flag indicates. Successful flanneling has neither of these features. It keeps one safe from penalties, so long as the levee of irony remains unbreached, and it preserves individualism.

Theater may also be used in evasion. The evader may have a set of cronies who form an appreciative audience for his cunning; or he may use elaborate displays of military enthusiasm, in order to conceal his depredations. But evasion itself, since it is covert, is not accomplished by the direct use of theater. Similarly, although open rebellion is generally accompanied by a performance that counters the official values by deliberately inverting them, the acts of defiance are situated squarely on the legal-rational side of organizational life; they break the rules and openly invite punishment. Only flanneling and other "Humbly report, sir" varieties of scrimshanking locate resistance entirely within the world of organizational enchantment, of the organization's own theatrical performances.

What advantages does the disengager get from this form of defiance? First, it is harder for the authorities to punish, because it presents itself ostensibly as the very reverse of a breach of regulations. But, if that were the main motivation, simple evasion would be a better tactic. Flanneling is a provocation, a form of mockery, an ironic defiance, and therefore dangerous. Evasion, on the other hand, does not provoke, does not court attention, is not a challenge, not insubordination, not defiance at all, but a concealed transgression of the organization's rules, and therefore potentially safer than flanneling. Evasion is prosaic, instrumental, scientific, and certainly intended to send messages to no one, except perhaps the offender himself and his fellow conspirators. But flanneling is different; it is an adventure, a challenge.

It is a challenge in two different senses. First it is an act of insubordination toward authorities, a deliberate ironic provocation. Second, it challenges the flanneler himself, because it calls for virtuosity; his performance is diminished and likely to be less effective if it has been wholly scripted beforehand. The flanneler extemporizes, adapting his act to the occasion; and the more subtle the adaptation, the better the performance. It is likely to fail if it is recognized as pure routine; there has to be an element of the individual in it, of the artist. The performance, while certainly drawing on established conventions, is creative, marking individuality. That is not the case with maneuvers on a drill square. They too are performances, theatrical, a spectacle both for the performers themselves and for anyone looking on. But they are collective, and whatever creative choreography may once have gone into them has long since been replaced by routine and convention; they are drills. Furthermore they are the theater of the organization, a celebration of its values. The flanneler's theatrical performances, on the other hand, are those of an individual, exercising initiative, extemporizing, taking risks, mocking organizational values, above all asserting the survival of his identity, proclaiming that, while he may be trapped within the body, he is not entirely of it.

But flannelers do more than that. They employ a curiously indirect logic against the organization's theater and its poetics. Direct logical refutation of a poetic truth, as I noted earlier, seems to miss the point, to be crass, having all the credibility of one who claims to have captured the experience of love in a chemical formula. Direct action. against flanneling, indicated by threats of punishment, although effective when it puts an end to the mockery, nevertheless acknowledges the kind of defeat that goes with backing out of a game when one is losing it. Theater that defies authority can only be contested, if the authority is not to lose face by changing the rules in midgame, by counterperformances of the same kind.[24]

The indirect logic, to which I referred, is a performance version of the logician's *reductio ad absurdum* (which is the valid deduction from a proposition of its own contradiction). In the strict sense, flanneling is not a matter of logic, since it does not involve propositions. But the "Humbly report, sir" performance, or any other sort of flanneling, makes a rule ridiculous, reduces it to absurdity, by obeying it mechanically as a machine would, and by not exercising the kind of discretion that a normal individual is expected to exercise. The irony is that the intention of the army's collective poetic performances is to do

[24]The constant abuse heaped on Svejk is a routinized counterpoetic, used by authorities to eradicate individualism. To the extent that it is routinized, it loses its edge. The riposte of the headmaster, who remarked that the Latin verses mocking him did not properly scan, was the more effective because it maintained the theatrical idiom.

exactly that, reduce individuals to being nonthinking components in an organizational machine.[25]

Flanneling also is a form of parody, of ridicule by imitation. From this aspect it is less an act of insubordination against authorities than a signaled disenchantment with an institution's theatrical presentation of itself. In my experience, as I said earlier, military theater effectively removed individuality, producing not-thinkers and inducing in them an overwhelming sense of belonging to the collectivity, even devotion. This was done by repetition. But the curve that plots the relationship between enchantment and repetition is bell shaped. A poem, if it is good, improves with repeated hearings, up to a point. The mind-bending effect of theatrical performances also are enhanced by repetition, but my memory is that the curve turns down. Military theater, for all but a few soldiers, eventually ceases to enchant, loses whatever meaning it once had, and becomes little more than "going through the motions." Drills—the pun is obligatory—are boring. When their sheer inanity bursts through into the individual's consciousness, they present themselves as nothing but idiotically tedious, enchanting only to an imbecile. Any routinized performance enforced by an organization, including those that purport not to be theater (what we call "red tape"), has that disenchanting quality. Flanneling is a performance that mimes exactly the message of disillusion: All this play acting is idiocy!

"Imbecility" returns us to Svejk, whose extravagant parodies of the army's theater officially proclaim that he is soft in the head. The irony of the situation, as I said, lies in the fact that the army itself, not Svejk, is idiotic. The army gets what it deserves, and Svejk's antics are no more than—to overwork the word—poetic justice. An imbecile is someone who is helpless, weak, or feeble. The army's aim (in the end self-defeating, I

[25]An analogous form of protest, this time in the prosaic area of organizational conduct, is working to rule.

will argue later) is to sterilize individualistic tendencies and make its soldiers strong only as members of the army's collectivities. Outside the collectivity the soldier is supposed to be helpless, an imbecile, and the army's poetic performances celebrate organizational power, collective strength, and individuals so dependent that they cease to be individuals. As individuals they are oafs and idiots and imbeciles; only within the collectivity can they assume the dignity of soldiers. This condition is signaled constantly and in many different ways, not least in the routine abuse that is heaped on the ordinary soldier by his superiors.[26] The result of thoroughgoing military poetic performances is not, however, to universalize the genuine imbecility that goes with being an automaton, but instead to make room for Svejk and other disengagers to assert themselves as individuals, by parodying their loyalty to the service, by parading a mock lack of individuality.

To assert individuality is at the same time to deny hierarchy, to deny the collectivity and the legitimacy of those who direct it. Armies are overwhelmingly paternalistic, sometimes nurturing, always guiding, and above all punishing. There is an element of paternalism in all organizations, even those like universities which claim to found themselves on the collegial principle of moral equality and to value the unrestricted development of *individual* talent. Equality in any shape is not a feature of formal military organization (although it can be salient in the informal side of a trooper's life); on the contrary, subordination is an endlessly repeated theme in military poetic performances. Svejk's acting out of imbecility has a wonderful double twist of meaning: through an ironic demonstration of addiction to hierarchy, it in effect proclaims his equivalence to those who abuse him as an imbecile, who are thereby them-

---

[26]In Svejk's army, unlike the army I knew, the abuse came as much from the officers as from the NCO's.

selves made imbeciles. Here, as a sample of his engaging lunacy, is Svejk explaining the need for military discipline:

> Our Lieutenant Makovec always used to say: "There's got to be discipline, you bloody fools, otherwise you'd be climbing about on the trees like monkeys, you god-forsaken idiots." And isn't that true? Just imagine a park, let's say at Charles Square, and on every tree an undisciplined soldier. It's enough to give you a nightmare! (Hasek 1973:8–9)

INSTITUTIONS ARE SLOW-WITTED

Why do organizations manage their theatrical confrontations with individuals badly? Anything can be parodied, but it is certainly easier to parody something that itself goes too far, that is repetitious, crass, boring, and irritating. Armies do licence theatrical inversions of military values on festive occasions, and sometimes turn a deaf ear to expressions of disenchantment, mockery, and disrespect in songs and chants and recitations, as I described earlier. But when authorities feel obliged to respond to individual poetic performances of disrespect, they usually find themselves compelled to move the encounter out of the theatrical style and into an instrumental mode. In other words all they can do is enforce compliance: they send Svejk to the garrison jail and they give enemas to malingerers (an act which, admittedly, is not without symbolic significance, even if that is not the intent). A theatrical response to the flanneler might seem more appropriate, but by their very nature organizations find it difficult to respond in that way.[27]

Why can the authorities not take precautions beforehand and

---

[27]The British army recognized its incapacity to deal on the same level with ironic performances and penalized them under the catch-all performative category of "dumb insolence."

so fine-tune their theater that they do not provoke ridicule and parody? Theater can be subtle; it can hint, be allusive, give an audience the quasi-creative joy of itself working out what the message is. The poetic performances of flanneling also have something of that delicate indirection, as when the officers perceive they are being mocked but cannot respond appropriately. Svejk's performance might then be called "pure poetry." But collective theater, mere spectacle, is not like that. If Svejk, the flanneler, is a ballerina (a strange thought), then collective poetic performances are soldiers in hobnailed boots, crashingly and repetitively asserting the superiority of the collectivity until the messages become meaningless, never delicate, never refined, never allusive. Collective poetic performances are all-or-nothing, and crudely so, spectacles intended to awe, even to intimidate. They do not lend themselves to subtlety, because the choreographers use the principle of the lowest common denominator and assume that both the audience and the performers are ordinary, crass, and insensitive Joes and Jills, anyone and everyone, including those with a tin ear and heavy on their feet.

But more than vulgarization is involved. The maintenance of a system of collective poetic performances is in the hands of a collectivity, in effect a hierarchy of elders obsessed with their dignity or, worse, of committees, which by their very nature are not programed to respond quickly to the unexpected. Collective decisions tend to be slow decisions. Decisions shunted up and down a hierarchy are also slow, and suffer from information-distortions. What is simple and straightforward and unsubtle and above all according to precedent is most easily transmitted. Under these conditions collective poetic performances are not only a vehicle for communication and the manipulation of others; they are also an indicator of a state of mind that makes it very understandable why those institutional economists who devise economic models of organizational behavior (described later) seem to embrace the concept of hierarchy without much ardor and appear keen to retain a place for the "rational" (self-interested) individual.[28]

That state of mind is inertia. A fearful stillness characterizes an overgrown bureaucracy, a stillness that is achieved by a quiet rejection of the organization's obligation to stay in touch with reality. Organizations tend to live within the walls of their own theatrical performances. Routinized repetitive activity, whether purportedly instrumental or avowedly expressive, becomes a statement of what the organization is, what it stands for, and what the standards are to which its members must conform. The window on the real world, to which the organization must adjust itself, is progressively obscured by poetically effective fantasies about the organization's identity; about its nature and importance. Such a system, if there is no intervention from outside, has positive feedback, growing off itself. Svejk's army, like many armies in the real world, came to exist more for itself and its rituals of deference and degradation, than to fight the nation's wars. All bureaucracies tend to slide down that particular slope.

Negative feedback may come directly from the outside world (wars get lost), or from inspections and reviews. In most large bureaucracies a cycle of sin and cleansing marks departure from, and return to, concern with the effective performance of the organization's task.[29] Flanneling also is a form of negative feedback, as are all forms of shirking, because they threaten institutional complacency. Flanneling, however, is a very distinctive kind of protest, not so much for the practical reason that it drives its victims—those in charge of the organization—out of their citadel of collective theatrical performances and into the efficient side of organizational discipline,

[28]See Chapter 4. These issues are more fully discussed in Bailey 1991b.
[29]The metaphor of alternating sin and penance is taken from Moore 1963:25.

but more for its nonviolent nondestructive assertion of individuality, and its reminder that no organization could survive if it managed to suppress individual initiatives entirely. Its esthetic appeal is its subtlety, the way it uses the disease itself to construct a therapy.

Chapter 4

Sidestepping Dignity

Jesus answered them and said, "Verily, verily, I say unto you, ye seek Me, not because ye saw the miracles, but because ye did eat of the loaves, and were filled."

—John 6:26

DEVOTION'S OTHER FACE

There is an ambitious theory that, in an almost allegorical form, explains how institutions, and the unequal distribution of power that they embody, come to exist. The mythmakers are economists wrestling with such concepts as *hierarchy*, or *ideology* or *institution*. Their problem is to reconcile the behavior that *hierarchy* describes with their own basic axiom, which is economic individualism. This axiom takes it for granted that people pursue their own interests and do so rationally; that is, they have sufficient information and sufficient powers of calculation to select the most efficient means to reach the chosen end, which is their own advantage.[1]

Economic individualism came under attack from several directions, including two from within economics itself. First, Herbert Simon and the behavioral economists pointed out that

[1]The emergence of these ideas is well described in Moe 1984.

most decisions are taken without rigorous calculation; out of habit, or copying the next person, or taking someone's advice. People do not optimize; they merely *satisfice*. Second, in 1937 Ronald Coase stirred the waters by foregrounding the fact that market principles (bargaining) do not much organize conduct *within* a firm, being replaced by a principle of hierarchy (command).

Hierarchy, in everyday discourse, has a whiff of morality; it suggests more than enforcement and a chain of command. It conveys also the idea of duty to a superior, whether an individual or an institution, and duty is something that must be done even if there is a loss in doing it. After Coase, economists had somehow to match the basic idea of an entirely rational (that is, self-interested) entrepreneur with the idea of duty. They did so in the following way.

Economic institutions—business large and small, engaged in profit making—function as a kind of suspended market. Other bureaucracies work that way too. People bargain for their best advantage, but they do not do it all the time. Those in charge (principals) conclude a contract with those whom they control (agents), agreeing what work will be done for what pay and in what conditions. Duty is then nothing beyond the obligation not to violate a contract. Interactions are essentially adversarial, but people cooperate for defined purposes and in defined ways, because they see an advantage in doing so. The notion of moral obligation—service given because it is intrinsically right to do so—is not required. The theory does not say that everyone in actuality behaves that way all the time, only that sufficient people do so sufficiently often to make the axiom useful for deductions about what is done or can be done or should be done in the real world.

Thus duty becomes a disguised form of self-interest. Coase himself made the idea economically palatable by showing that hierarchy, defined in this fashion, was economically rational; its function is to reduce transaction costs. The agent does not bargain over every interaction with his principal, because he and the principal have a mutually advantageous contractual agreement covering all interactions of a specified kind; thus the costs of their interaction are reduced. Thus also hierarchy is construed as a form of contract and the paradigm of economic individualism (with the principal standing in, as a quasi individual, for the hierarchy) is preserved.

With help from Adam Smith, this theory can be expanded to account for the entire evolutionary history of human society.[2] In the past our ancestors were poorer than we are because they did not know how to trade. When there is trade, producers can specialize, advance their technology, and profit from economies of scale, producing greater quantities at lower cost. But trade requires trust that the trading partners will do what they promise. If there are connections already in existence—if, for example, the other person is a kinsman, or a *paesano*, or of the same religion—then trust is strengthened. But these connections still keep the scale of operations small because institutions like kinship or neighborliness or religion are themselves of narrow range, leaving untapped the trade that might have been done with strangers. In any case these institutions are apt to regard money-making transactions carried on within their essentially moral framework as parasitical.

Clearly the need is for an institution that is exclusively economic in its purpose—concerned only with the production, distribution, and consumption of wealth—yet has the ability to inspire trust. The trust, moreover, should not rest on personal ties. It should be impersonal, the same for everyone, status-free, a world where business is business, and efficiency (measured by profit) is the only criterion for making a transaction. But how can one trust a stranger whose only motive is his own advantage? The solution is a third party acting as guarantor. So goods come with brand names that serve as guarantees of

[2]A brief and clear example of this argument is North 1989.

quality, and practitioners are licensed by guilds or by the state, and one deals through banks rather than directly with unknown trading partners, because the bank oversees the transaction. The point, of course, is that without this third party we would have to do the reliability research ourselves, and that might well be prohibitively expensive. In other words, the institutional third party—the contract enforced by law and the state—lowers the cost of transactions, and so trade can expand and we all are better off.

But this vision of infinite wealth recedes as one encounters reality. The reality is that those who guarantee the honesty of status-free exchanges are themselves liable to be corrupted by the status they hold. Who will watch the watchmen? Means triumph over ends and the custodians busy themselves with enhancing power instead of using it to further trade. Regulation becomes an end in itself and sometimes also a profitable business for the regulators. The disinterested concern for the public good that the evolutionary theory suggests should be characteristic of institutions is replaced by an interest in power. Hegemony diminishes, obedience is exacted through force and fraud, and disengagement deals in the same coin, becoming practical.

None of this falsifies the central assumption of the evolutionary model: that human societies have become more and more complex, and that this complexity has been the means to produce larger amounts of wealth. But, as the complexity and scope of institutions rise, so also do power and the level of mistrust. The bigger and more comprehensive the organizing institution, the greater the difference in power between those who give orders and those who obey them. At the same time the trust that can exist between people who know one another face to face declines. Since the subjects are mistrustful, they assume that the organization is taking more than it is giving, and they shirk or cheat over the tasks that the authorities expect them to perform. Alternatively they go in for symbolic acts of insubordination that serve to reassure them that the organization does not deserve the respect that it demands. In turn these forms of disengagement cause an intensification of reward and punishment, intended to discourage shirking, or, alternatively, a greater investment in hegemony through the manufacture of devotion.

At several points in this hypothetical evolution, disengagement is likely to occur. Mistrust alone, produced by impersonal interactions, is enough to start the process. Work extracted only by the threat of punishment, mere compliance, should be less efficient, other things being equal, than work willingly done. If you do not know that cooperation enhances productivity, or do not believe it, or believe it but also believe that the increased wealth will not be equitably shared, then it is rational to resist organization and to compete for a better share of the existing stock of wealth.

This chapter will discuss practical disengagement, setting it in the framework of the evolutionary model of an increasingly complex social order. As the mechanisms intended to impose order change, so also do the methods of practical disengagement. I will proceed by comparing practical disengagement in peasant societies and in industrial societies.

PEASANTS AND WORKERS

Until about fifty years ago the history of peasant societies was written mainly from the top downward. Historians were interested in nations and their politics and they focused on people in power. The history of Britain and of other European countries that a schoolboy learned was the history of kings and nobles, and if the common people made an appearance at all, it was only as those whose labors and suffering made possible the deeds of their rulers. Only in occasional and invariably disastrous rebellions did peasants make their mark on that kind of history.

The structure of peasant society was in the main feudal, but with certain nonfeudal accretions. A model feudal society separates nobles from commoners, the former as rulers, the latter as subjects. The nobles are themselves divided in two ways. First they are ranked, a king at the top and below him lords who owe allegiance to the king as his vassals, and lesser lords who are the vassals of those lords, and so on downward through the nobility. But this vertical arrangement is unstable, because the nobles are also divided by competition. A senior lord might try to displace the king, and so on all the way down the hierarchy of nobles. These challenges are made easier because each lord is, notionally at least, politically and economically self-contained on his own domain. A king has no apparatus, neither economic nor political, that would let him interfere within the domain of the lord who owes him allegiance. Nor can those lords interfere in the domains of their vassals. The effect is to create a very unstable conflict-ridden political society made up of relatively small, highly independent inward-looking, self-contained units, interacting mainly through the interactions of their rulers. The nation (if one can call it that) then becomes an arena in which the nobles fight it out with one another for a position at the top of the highest accessible heap.

If one steps further back in order to observe change, one can discern a process that is caught by the evolutionary model set out earlier. From this perspective what went on in the arena was not simply a series of contests for first place, but also a process in which those who could stabilize their exchanges with others increased their power. To the extent that any king or lord could govern not through lesser clones of himself (his vassals) but through specialized agents, who could never themselves be his rivals because they were specialized in only one of the functions of government (justice, finance, and so on), he made his position more secure. Consequently the reality of government at all levels of feudal society was not simply the feudal ideal of the lord, but rather of a lord with his specialized servants, who were in charge of revenue or of spiritual matters or of law and order or whatever else.

The function of these officials was to enhance the king's ability to control his people. They made more efficient the king's capacity to intrude into the lives of his peasants, to collect tribute, to impress young men into his armies, and to punish those who opposed him and remove those who stood in his way. When peasants did rise in rebellion, usually their first and most brutally treated victims were the officials in charge of the law, and sometimes the clergy. Sometimes also the king could present himself as the champion of the poor people against oppressive officials and extortionate clergy.

The state, from this elevated point of view, was not the entire population, but only those who governed. From below, where the peasants were, the state was an instrument of oppression and exploitation, tempered by its somewhat unreliable provision of law and order, which in practice often amounted to no more than a racket; the rulers protected their citizens from other rulers by themselves monopolizing extortion. From the rulers' point of view peasants were instruments to be used in the struggle for power that went on between nobles in the state and between states. Peasants produced the wealth that paid for the state and its ambitions, and for the clergy and the religious institutions, most of which were no less predatory on the peasants than was the state itself.

What kind of persons are peasants? Their basic economic unit is the family, and the first priority that peasants use to guide their decisions is the family's continuity and viability, not, as with a business, profit. One can sell out a business for a profit; one should not sell out a family. A proper peasant head of household will pass up the chance to make more money, if by doing so he would drive his sons off the farm. In the language of economists, the viability of the household is the peasant's main utility function. To a smaller and much debated extent, the viability of the peasant *community* is also part of their utility function.

Peasant *society* divides itself into peasants and their communities on the one side, and on the other their exploiters, who are the gentry, the clergy, the merchants, and townspeople in general. The exploiters are better organized than the peasants, having readier access to coercive instruments, which culminate in the state. On the other hand exploitation is a secondary, if necessary, endeavor; the game that matters for the exploiters is the one that they play against each other. This factional instability much diminishes the control the rulers have over their peasants, who, on occasions, can profit by playing off one lord against another, or a lord against a bishop. Peasants live out their lives devising ways to protect themselves and their households from the predatory incursions of the state, while the state is organized, albeit inefficiently, to extract as much as it can from the peasants.[3]

This model of peasant society centers upon the notion of power and resistance to power. Anything that diminishes the self-sufficiency of the peasant household—markets, taxes, specialized skills or goods that the peasant needs but cannot provide for himself, impressment into armies, and most of all the free flow of information upward—represents a victory for the state and a defeat for the peasants. The situation is that of a zero-sum game, pointed not at increasing the general wealth by cooperation in productive activities, expanding the scale of exchange, increasing specialization, encouraging technical advancement, and so forth, but instead at fighting over the division of an existing stock of wealth.

[3]An informative account of the shelter that factionalism among rulers provided for Southeast Asian peasants is to be found in Adas 1981:219–26.

In this fight the peasants' main weapon is one or another form of disengagement. In the peasant world everything points inward, making small worlds of household and village community, building barriers against outside contacts and outside ideas, fearful of strangers and strange ideas, neither searching out new knowledge nor thinking about progress. As a consequence, peasant life, in a way analogous to that of the rulers, is lived in small parcels, each walled off from its neighbors. Peasants' concern is for their families and, to a lesser extent, for their communities. The peasantry as a social category commands only a little of their awareness and less of their concern, for beyond the community and its neighbors are strangers who by definition are threatening; at least they are not part of a community that deserves moral consideration, and the community marks a boundary where normal human kindness ends. Peasants, Marx said, are potatoes in a sack; separate unorganized individual entities. They fear what is strange and they fear what is new. But they are not uncalculating; when they do enter the market, they are proverbially hard bargainers. The guiding notion is that beyond their own community (and sometimes within it) if one is not a victimizer, then one must be a victim.

This, of course, is a model, and a design for hardheaded disengagement. In actuality peasant households and peasant communities were caught within revenue-exacting states and never were able to achieve the desired total self-sufficiency. Peasants also learned to want goods that they could not make themselves and so came to patronize markets, and therefore had to produce for markets as well as for the state. Peasant societies and cultures constitute, as Robert Redfield put it, part-societies and part-cultures, trying but always failing to be complete in themselves.[4]

Nevertheless, to a degree peasants did manage to keep the

[4]Redfield 1956:20.

state and its agents at arm's length. They did so in a variety of practical ways that involved concealment, evasion, lying, and creating a confusion in which they could hide their property and themselves. They poached game from the fields and the forests and fish from the streams. They stole wood from state forests. When they paid tribute in grain, they paid it with the worst quality and mixed in stones and dirt to increase the bulk. When they could use the law, they did so, not so much by going to court, but simply by taking what they wanted and, when challenged, pointing to a regulation that arguably justified what they had done. There is an entertaining account in Scott (1987) of the latitude French peasants made for themselves from the fact that custom prevailed over the canon law that stipulated tithing (payment of one-tenth of the *gross* crop to ecclesiastical authorities), and of how they exploited loopholes in the law. Garden crops were exempt from tithes, with the result that gardens expanded to cover most of the holding. The sheaves at the base of a stack were not reckoned for tithe, so that stacks came to have an oddly flattened profile. On the excuse of bad weather or of rumors about thieves in the neighborhood, the harvest was gathered and threshed (and a portion of it hidden away) before the collecting agent could arrive to make the count and take his share. All these kinds of things were done without any formal organization or any overt conspiracy; there was no need for that, since disengagement was a way of life. It was also very effective. Writing in the same essay about an Islamic tithe in Malaya, Scott reckoned that evasive measures achieved a 90 percent reduction in the amount paid over to the clerical authorities.

Practical disengagement is an eminently realistic strategy for peasants, given the predatory nature of the state. From time to time peasant societies were racked by rebellions, wars conducted on both sides with exemplary brutality;[5] some peasants

---

[5]There are some vivid descriptions in Tuchman 1979.

took to banditry.[6] All peasants continuously resorted to the less dangerous forms of practical resistance like those described above, using the strategy of evasion and a low profile: stealing the lord's property and cheating his agents, avoiding contact, maintaining a humble demeanor when in contact with the strong, concealing whatever wealth they possessed, and mitigating hardship by maintaining a habit of frugality. In such an ambience, practical resistance in the form of theft, cheating and other forms of evasion is a very rational strategy.

Urban industrial workers had what peasants did not: an economic environment that forced them into organized opposition and, eventually, into unionization and political mobilization, thus making possible concerted pressure on governments and the dominant classes.

Peasants created fantasies of the world turned upside down, the donkey riding on its master and the hare chasing the hounds. Marx also had a fantasy, not of an inverted world but of a world without domination. Lenin, a firm centralist, had no such illusions and neither, I believe, do most workers. The reality they envision is neither themselves as master, nor the disappearance of masters, but of a master constrained into giving a bigger share of his wealth to those who did his work. The vision is not black and white, extremes that lend themselves to dramatic portrayal of an inverted hierarchy or of everyone made equal (as in heaven), but a compromise that could be made into a reality, with no need or room for fantasy.

The peasant household aimed for self-sufficiency (within the peasant community), to support itself materially and to prevent, as far as possible, political and economic incursions by gentry and clergy. (The ruling class depended for its existence on making those same incursions.) An industrial worker cannot

[6]Hobsbawm 1959 and 1969.

see the world in the way peasants did; a worker needs the job and he needs the boss. A world without bosses or a world in which he or those like him are the bosses is seen as a dream world. Workers cannot afford to close down the exchanges they make with the bosses. The realistic strategy is to make those exchanges less unfavorable, either overtly through political action, or covertly through practical disengagement.

Peasants too are caught in a net of domination, but the workers' net has a finer mesh. The rulers of a peasant society are like marauders who make periodical descents on their victims, take what they want, and then go away. They have no direct hand in *production*. Industrial masters are different; they monitor; they are constantly vigilant, constantly intervening.[7] They do not simply take what is produced; they supervise the process of production itself by means of a complex and intrusive chain of command. This command structure, however, has entailments that from the point of view of the masters are unfortunate. It requires that they share with at least some of the workers a politically crucial skill that formerly they monopolized; that is, literacy.[8] Industrial workers are more efficient if they can read and write and follow standardized procedures that are objectified and communicated in writing. The same literacy that gives individuals a measure of autonomy also makes it possible for them to combine for political opposition against their masters. Continued conflict, as has often been said, makes antagonists resemble one another; trade union bosses come to use the same tactics and have the same values and even begin to look like their managerial opponents. Workers and management may be enemies and see themselves

[7]This statement is generally accurate, but does not convey the wide variation in degree and technique of managerial supervision found at different times and in different places. See Burawoy 1985.

[8]See Gellner 1989.

engaged in zero-sum conflict (even when they need not be), but culturally they have much more in common than do peasants and gentry.

What place is there in this model for cheating or shirking, for the simple evasion of the duties or regulations that are imposed by the masters on the rank and file? The same industrial environment that eventually taught workers the skills required for organized opposition also made possible a huge and ingenious repertoire for shirking and cheating and covertly extracting from the organization benefits that it does not want to give. Industrial bureaucracies have highly developed mechanisms for monitoring performance. Any rational enterprise, whether manufacturing, commercial, or governmental, has built into it systems of accounting, of making sure that people do what they are hired to do: supervisors, time clocks, quality control, bonuses and penalties, and the like. Furthermore, specialization makes one segment of an enterprise dependent on the performance of others, so that the failure of one part affects all parts and thus becomes more visible. Such features call for more ingenuity on the part of those who decide to cheat the organization or not to give it all that it wants from them. The proposition is simple: the more varied and complex the regulations, the greater the opportunity for defeating them, and the more complicated the methods of cheating and shirking. Practical resistance, other things being equal, increases in proportion to the complexity not only of the organization in general, but also of the measures specifically intended to prevent rule breaking. For an example, let us look at piecework in an American factory (Roy 1955).[9]

Five kinds of actor must be presented to make this form of practical disengagement comprehensible. First, there are machinists who turn out a small component that will be put into some larger component by workers on a production line, and

_____

[9]The same factory, a generation later, is described in Burawoy 1985.

so on upward until eventually a completed product emerges. The component is shaped from a casting that someone else has made, and the machinists work on it to give it the precise dimensions required. The machine can be fitted with the appropriate jigs and dies that control the contours of the product and reduce the need for operator-skill. Machinists have nothing to do with the design; nor are they involved in the manufacturing process before the component comes to them or after it leaves them. They make the same kinds of pieces all day long, day after day. They do not even set the machine up with the jigs and dies; that is done by a specialized setup person, who reads the blueprints and determines what parts must be fitted to the machine to do this particular job. The third person is an inspector, who examines a sample of the finished products, to make sure they meet the specifications. Fourth, there are storeroom personnel, from whom the material to be processed must be collected, and who find from their shelves whatever drill bits, dies, jigs, and so forth the setup person determines are necessary. These are all shop-floor personnel, under the general control of supervisors and foremen.

The fifth person belongs not to the shop floor but to management, being described as management's "hatchet man." This is the time-and-motion expert. When a new component is first made, the process is subjected to a time-and-motion study. The machine is set up and then an operator uses it to produce components under the expert's eye. The expert has two functions; one is to suggest more efficient ways for the worker to do that particular job. The other task, and in this context the more salient, is to determine a base rate; that is, how many pieces the worker should produce in an hour. Suppose the figure is 100. If the worker produces 100, he will be paid the basic wage rate, which has already been negotiated through collective bargaining. If he produces 125 pieces in the hour, he will receive 25 percent extra wage for that hour.

Work at the machine is classified into four categories. One is the time-and-motion study, done under the eye of the expert; a second is the setup, carried out under the direction of the setup person, and including time spent in collecting material and tools from the storeroom; a third is rework, done on those pieces that the inspector has rejected but which are judged salvageable; and the fourth is piecework. The first three kinds of work are paid at the basic wage rate; piecework offers the chance of earning more.

It does not take much imagination to see that this arrangement in practice will not turn out to be what was intended, a beautifully logical way to motivate workers into using their time and energy to maximize production in a spirit of cooperation. Instead it is an inevitable maker of mistrust and deceit and bad faith. The time-and-motion expert is on the watch for tricks; the operator is out to trick him. But if the operator succeeds, and later the managers find that operators are regularly producing at twice the basic rate, all they need do is raise the rate. Workers then get the feeling that they have to run faster to stay where they are. An adversarial spirit and the need to deceive—to define the situation to one's own advantage—are built into the entire system.

To make the system work to their own advantage, workers need to control the access that management has to information about what operators are actually doing at any particular time. If time that is officially recorded at the basic rate (setup, rework, or time-and-motion) can in fact be spent on producing pieces, the operator wins. Pieces made then can be covertly added to whatever is produced during "honest" piecework time. Sometimes this is done, at some risk, merely by altering the figures on the time sheet. More often, it seems, the shop-floor people, the inspectors, storeroom people, setup men (but never the time-and-motion expert), collude in devising "make-up angles" that will turn jobs that would have been "stinkers" into "gravy jobs." Even the foreman advises, "You've got to chisel a little around here to make money." More on this topic later, for it raises again the possibility that there can be a moral community of disengagers, an idea that does not sit well with the basic axiom of economic individualism.

Notice how different this world is from that of the peasant. Management is intimately involved in the productive process, and the complexity of regulation entailed in such involvement provides the opportunity that the worker needs to disengage effectively. Notice also how different the work is. Industrial work of this kind and at this level is broken into tiny fragments, effectively squashing any creative satisfaction, and making for alienation, a sense that the self has been lost in an organization. Notice, third, how much brain power goes into manipulating people, constraining them so that they have no choice but to do what the firm wants them to do, turning them, in fact, into an appendage of the machines they operate. The workers, correspondingly, put their energies into modifying the situation so that they retain some control over it. Somehow the focus has slipped from productivity to power.

Nor is this continuation of politics by other means peculiar to the free-enterprise manufacturing world. Miklos Haraszti (1977) wrote about piece rates in a Hungarian tractor factory. There too norms are set by time-study people and machine operators work out various dodges to get the maximum on piece rates. The stratagems that Haraszti describes (called "looting") are mostly technical, for example setting the machine to take a larger cut than is prescribed, and so completing an operation in one pass instead of two or three. This makes for a short life for cutting edges and machining heads, but it does save time for the operator. Time is also saved when the operator, instead of clamping the piece in the machine, holds it in place, thus risking the loss of fingers. These and other shortcuts raise output. But management keeps a record, and when they decide they are paying out too much, they raise the norm again. This, in turn, sets the workers to finding new devices to beat the system, and both sides are off into an entropic Derby that can be ended only by industrial action of some sort. That is the point at which the safety valve of beating the system sticks.

There are some interesting differences in tone between this book and the essay on the American factory that focused on manipulating what gets recorded on the time sheets. There is no love lost in the American factory between management (especially the time-and-motion experts) and the shop-floor people, but one puts the essay down with a sense that one has been reading a handbook on how to win at chess. Alternatively, the essay exudes the calm acceptance of Vinnie the barman, who knows that the whole story is "screw them because they are screwing you." The Hungarian book, in contrast, is an impassioned account of injustice. Its tone is moralistic in the extreme, and its theme is not so much cheating, but the exploitation that causes workers to cheat.[10]

> He who sells his time, his strength, his abilities for wages, whether bit-by-bit for piece-rates or in a more transparent total form, knows that he does not work for himself. He knows that he has sold everything, including his right to determine how much he will produce. . . . The norm is the thinly veiled constraint within the apparently voluntary framework of wage labour. Incessantly it reminds those who dream of a fair wage of the true nature of wage labour, so that as a result of the constant threat to our conditions of life, we "freely" pave the way to ever-growing output. (Haraszti 1977:131)

Notice again that power is the issue, not productivity. Later Haraszti remarks how he had always wanted to follow the pieces he made and see them emerge as part of a tractor.

---

[10]Haraszti was put on trial for writing it. For an informative and somewhat corrective commentary on the context and on the book itself see Burawoy 1985.

That wouldn't change much, but at least it would allow me to check a few of the things they throw in our faces as irrefutable arguments when we are given orders. If we could all do this, they couldn't shut us up with: "That's the way it is; there's no alternative." (1977:147)

Notice also that the power involved is not only the power to answer back but also the power of symbolic disengagement: the right to preserve one's identity from total alienation to the organization, to the collectivity.

The technology of the norms is a miraculous technology. From the labor of those who know only its fragments, it welds a totality; and it realizes a finished product from the labour of men who do not know the purpose, either of the product, or of their own labour and whose aim is to maintain their own existence. (1977:130–31)

The same theme, discontent as the product of meaningless work, is caught in "homers" (1977:138–46). Homers are complete products made on the machines by the worker for his own satisfaction: a part for a tap in the kitchen at home, rulers, pencil boxes, ashtrays, keyholders, and the like. They are not for sale. They are made from scrap. Making them does not even rob the organization of the worker's time, since he is not paid while making them.

But this time on the machine is stolen, and making homers is against regulations and must be done covertly. Therefore it is practical disengagement, evasion. But the reward is not practical; it is symbolic and reflexive—"the joy of . . . unity between conception and execution" (1977:142), of designing and making a whole thing. So the operators "win back power over and freedom from the machine." One can see in the making of homers some resemblance to flanneling, the joy of being creative and spontaneous in the teeth of an institution that suppresses both these qualities. The workers produce "useless things" and they "renounce payment," thus also renouncing economic rationality. Like Svejk they are sending a message about human dignity both to the authorities and to themselves.

Finally, the workers collude with one another, not only by looking the other way when they see regulations being broken, but also sometimes, to get a "homer" finished, helping each other out on their different machines. Here again, as in the collusion on the American shop floor, disengagement reveals itself as in part a cooperative practice in the context of a moral community.

GUMS AND SCHOLARS

I now shift the scene far away from the factory floor, where people are presented as mostly thinking about how much they can get into their wage packet and how little work they need give in return, to another world that is forever canting about service and duty, where work is styled a privilege. The setting is that same university in Britain, where the "new map of learning" was being followed, and nothing was good that did not depart from the "Germanic" pattern, and only slackers refused to go the extra mile. Quite soon experience dampened enthusiasm, the arteries hardened, reality testing was no longer branded negativism, and the vibrant tones of those who asked "What fine thing shall we do next?" were replaced, or at least followed, by dourer voices asking "What can we afford to do?" But even into the time of realism, when it was clear that uninhibited brainstorming and mutual shaming to go that extra mile were mostly just talk and certainly no substitute for books in the library or other academic necessities, there survived a morally prescriptive stereotype of what was called the "Good University Man." (The irreverent lost no time in reducing that to its acronym GUM, and also put into circulation another not-inappropriate acronym for the Bad University Man.)

GUMs were not distinguished from the rest of the faculty by the brilliance of their scholarship or the effectiveness of their teaching (*everyone*, by virtue of belonging to that institution, was *ipso facto* a fine scholar and an exceptionally devoted and talented teacher). Rather they were characterized first by their total acceptance of the institution's philosophy and second by dedicated service to the *management* of the institution.

GUMs accepted the philosophy of the new map of learning—they even got together and wrote a book about it (Daiches 1964)—but, paradoxically, the real GUM, while certainly putting the advancement of knowledge well behind the dissemination of wisdom, put in only a little service in the classroom and a lot of service in committee rooms. To spend time and effort making one's name in the world of research and scholarship was to be what about that time began to be called a "free rider." I once heard a dean castigate a young woman (a philosopher widely considered a Good University Person and an inspiring teacher), because she had requested unpaid leave to write a book. There would be opportunity enough for that, he said, if ever she qualified herself for sabbatical leave (for which, as it happened, that university at that time made no provision); meanwhile the continued success of the institution required her continuous presence. Service was a privilege and its own reward; her desire to advance herself showed a regrettable lack of public spirit.

The dean's attitude toward the philosopher and her scholarly ambitions was extreme, and it may have been a hangover from his formative years as an educator. Before dedicating himself relatively late in life to the university, he had been headmaster of a boy's school, an ancient and renowned foundation, which, like most of its peers, taught that character came before brains, and that devotion to the institution itself, and to the nation, was the highest of virtues. In fact, that is what "virtue" meant, holding one's own interests second to the interests of the collectivity.

Notice that there are two meanings compounded in the word "institution." First, the university is an institution in the sense that it is a legally recognized corporation, controlling property, making contracts with its employees and others, both restrained by law and possessing its own coercive sanctions by virtue of its legal standing. Its employees, including faculty members, must live by its regulations and provide it with the services for which they were hired. In return the institution gives them a salary and various other perquisites, and, like the larger society around it, makes possible an ordered, nonchaotic existence, without which life would be intolerable.

The institution that the dean had in mind was not this impersonal legal entity that owns property, makes contracts and provides a framework for ordered interaction, and is in the end nothing more than a formal organization, an instrument for accomplishing certain defined tasks (in this case education and research). The university, as the dean saw it, was not a contractual entity at all, but one that bound in its members by tacit convention or by solemn covenant, or perhaps in a fashion that needed no explicit agreement because they were "of the body." The university was not an instrument but an end in itself, having a status that was not legal, but moral. The faculty were not just employees, but together they constituted a collectivity, a collegial body, the members of which had obligations toward one another that were founded on the same kind of moral imperative that is supposed to hold together, for example, a group of kin or a fellowship of true-believers. That was the community that GUMs served, and on which BUMs took their "free ride."

The mark of a GUM, as I said, is that he (or she) stands ready to undertake managerial tasks "beyond the call of duty" and is apparently willing to put his own interests second to those of the university. But that only talks about his purport-edly benignant attitude; it does not say what in fact he does. What he does is serve on committees and do the work that committee service requires: reading documents, writing posi-tion papers, debating, making decisions, and persuading others of the rightness of those decisions. The decisions may be rou-tine: examination boards, space allocation committees, appoint-ment and promotion boards, and so forth. Alternatively they may respond to emergencies: rebellious students, inadequate funds for recreational activities, books stolen from the library, and a thousand other things.

Solving either kind of problem, crisis or routine, constitutes a public service, because all those in the university who enjoy the benefit of a successful solution do so whether they made a contribution to it or not. The good that emerges is not privatiz-able; those who fail to pay their pound of flesh, in the form of committee service, still get the benefits. This fact is well known, and the cordial contempt that ordinary academics usu-ally feel for assiduous committeemen may be tempered with a remark like "Well, someone has to do it, and sooner him than me!"

But why does someone—that is, one of "us"—have to do it? Why should the moral collectivity become involved? Why not leave it to be done by the university in its status of legal entity? The usual answer is that the university as a corporation is man-aged by professional administrators who are not competent to make decisions about student examinations, or faculty promo-tions, or other academic matters, and are too remote to under-stand what is troubling the students or what students need, or why the university would or would not be better off without teachers of philosophy. More important, the administrators are at best only marginally part of the moral collectivity. They are outsiders who do not understand the mysteries of academic life and do not share in its grace. They are not really "of the body."

That simple answer correctly describes the views of most faculty members. But it is incomplete, because it does not say plainly that to leave such decisions to professional administrators would be to surrender academic autonomy. Nor does it come to the fundamental dilemma that membership of collectivities everywhere presents to us: we desire both freedom and order, and are reluctant to admit that these are in complementary distribution with one another. As individuals we appreciate the provision of order and are grateful to institutions (in their legal guise), so long as they stay where we think they belong. But organizations sometimes seem to become rapacious, expanding, wanting more and more, asking ever more frequently for "the extra mile." They dominate and control, rewarding, punishing, restricting information with rules of confidentiality, making us not members but subjects. Then we resent them, and if we are bold we protest openly, and if we are less bold we keep a low profile, hoping that our failure to go the extra mile will not be noticed, thus selecting evasion before defiance. The dilemma is ours, not the organization's. The organization only wants order (and, of course, our unquestioning commitment) and generally considers what we call "freedom" a form of irresponsibility and even sinful. But we want both order and freedom (the right to withhold commitment) and we refuse to acknowledge that those two things get in each other's way.

From this point of view the public good that GUMs provide looks like nothing less than freedom; our chance to govern our own lives. GUMs are part of our moral community, supposedly; and they undertake, on everyone's behalf, the burden of managing its affairs. The professional administrators are then our servants and we are a self-governing collegial body. GUMs mediate the contradiction between freedom and order; they resolve the dilemma; they give us our freedom.

If that extravagant claim is true, then why are GUMs so often held in low regard by their colleagues, or at least ambiva-

lently judged? The best they often get is the grudging acknowledgment that the job has to be done and is difficult and
time-consuming. More often they encounter derision, contempt, suspicion, and even fear. Contempt is manifested in the
frequent charge—sometimes a canard—that GUMs do what
they do because they have nothing left to contribute to scholarship. So they keep themselves busy, talking endlessly and
mostly pointlessly, pretending to responsibility while the place
is in fact run by a few powerful administrators.

But why should anyone be afraid of a harmless busybody or
a failed academic? The answer is that they seem harmless only
so long as one accepts the myth that power is not an issue in a
university, that it is transcended by other higher values, just as
in an economic enterprise power is supposed to take second
place to productivity. But in fact organizations are not simple
collectivities in which the members stand equal in dignity; organizations are of necessity structured by inequality. Power is
a concept about which the dean is required by the logic of his
position to be disingenuous, because power goes with conflict,
and conflict has no place in his definition of an institution. But
ordinary Jill and ordinary Joe in academia are ambivalently
cautious in their dealings with GUMs, because not all of them
are harmless. Some have power and use it to hurt their enemies
and help their friends.

From this perspective GUMs are not seen as noble and un-
selfish individuals who mediate the contradiction between freedom and order and so allow "us" to exercise our democratic
rights and govern ourselves. Instead GUMs are renegades, no
longer collegial equals, no longer with "us," no longer genuine
scholars, but power-hungry people who have sold out and al-
lied themselves with a ruling group, the "them" who govern
and exploit "us."

This discussion has modified the dean's image of a university
and made it not unlike the shop floor, the GUM standing in
for the time-and-motion expert who sets the "norm" of right

conduct in the organization. But, as will become clear, practical disengagement in an academic setting is a much less straightforward affair than it is in the factory, mostly because the idea of money-for-services-rendered is vastly confused in academia by ideas of duty and the question of where duty is owed.

Before I joined the dean's university, I taught in a pleasant academic enclave located within an institution that was much larger and much older than the dean's place. It was run by a combination of an iron-bound bureaucracy and a no less rigid ideology. The bureaucracy was gigantic and ubiquitous, all precedents seemingly having long been set. Like all bureaucracies it went in for some mystification of itself (especially of how it in fact worked) and one had access to its favors through the services of administrative vicars. They were a humdrum lot, and obliging, most of them either elderly ladies or retired colonial civil servants, not by any stretch of the imagination like prophets; they kept a low profile. Like the bureaucracy itself, they were taken for granted, beyond ordinary understanding, but certainly not such as to inspire awe, merely a familiar and reassuring part of the landscape.

The bureaucracy functioned very predictably and for the most part effectively at doing what, over the years, it had grown into doing, which was to service the needs of the individual scholar. Everyone, of whatever rank—assistant lecturer, lecturer, senior lecturer, reader, or professor—considered himself unique and exceptional, and gloried in the fact. It was indeed a place where the rhetoric of the dean—service to the institution is all—would have gotten short shrift. (It was also one of the places from which the dean's university took care to distinguish itself.)

Of course there had to be some service: examination boards, appointment boards, the heads of departments meeting with the director of the institution to divide space and other resources, a committee to run the common room and decide which kind of biscuits should be sold with morning coffee or afternoon tea, the perennial routine of housekeeping that characterizes any such institution. But precedent took care of most matters, because nothing much came up that was new (certainly in comparison with the dean's university), and the professional administrators in the registrar's and bursar's offices made sure that the various facilities, academic and otherwise, were efficiently managed. There were a few GUMs, assiduous committee men; they were not held in high esteem, although it was agreed that they did a lot of work, some of it necessary. The "genuine scholars" rarely volunteered for committee work, and when they did the regular members wished they had stayed away, for most of them had the unfortunate habit of indulging to the full the scholar's propensity for quibbling over detail, making committee work an intellectual sport rather than an occasion on which to make necessary decisions.

These individual scholars never thought they were shirking their duty and would never have described themselves as svejks; they would have thought the comparison insulting. But, if I recall some of the behavior I observed (and leave unconsidered for the moment the question of motivation), what they did, and what the institution itself did, seem to have something in common with Svejk.

The institution's speciality was expertise in foreign languages and cultures of a particular kind: those which were remote, out of the ordinary, and supposedly unfamiliar to mainstream British and European scholarship. Tibetan, Korean, the languages of China, Japanese, dead languages such as Accadian or Sanscrit, the tribal languages of Africa, the languages of contemporary South Asia, Arabic, Georgian, and the less familiar languages of the Soviet Union are representative examples. Those languages, together with the cultures and histories of the people who spoke or had spoken them, represented the institution's intellectual concentration. The 1939–45 war had uncovered a national ignorance of such matters, and, presumably for reasons of national security, postwar governments considerably increased the funding of the institution.

The governments of the time, Conservative and Labour alike, had certain expectations about how the money would be used, but (as was not the case in Mrs. Thatcher's Britain) the politicians and their civil servants hesitated to say exactly what they wanted and to prescribe in any detail what scholars should investigate; in any case they had no finely tuned monitoring apparatus. The result can fairly be described as institutional svejkism. The study of Accadian, from any point of view, can hardly be a contribution to national security. Knowledge of the languages of India might be so considered, but surely not a life spent in the loving exegesis of fourteenth-century Tamil devotional poetry. Swahili, a dominant language of eastern central Africa, could surely be of strategic significance, but it would be difficult to say the same of a definitive account of the work of certain Swahili poets on the small Kenyan island of Lamu. In other words, these scholars were, with the support of the institution, able to channel institutional resources into doing what they themselves personally thought should be done.

Some individuals followed a similar course in evading their institutional obligations. For example, it was the custom to avoid students, so far as was possible, especially undergraduate students. Fortunately the demand for undergraduate teaching in the institution's specialities was not large. Even postgraduates were not plentiful: in those days Orientalists and Africanists were second-class citizens in academia, and a historian, for example, could earn a better reputation by publishing a few essays on the port records of Liverpool than by writing exemplary histories of the Mughal empire or of Arab influences on Africa's eastern coast. But occasionally someone came along determined to take a degree, or at least follow a course, in one or another exotic language. It was then considered only prudent, by certain teachers, to stay away from the institution for the first week or ten days of the term, in the hope that any prospective student would lose heart and look for another language, thus inflicting himself on some other teacher, who had not been canny enough to make himself unavailable. Thus time was preserved for scholarship, and—as it was humorously remarked of one senior man—the only student the professor would accept was the student who would eventually succeed him in the professorship.

That is enough to set the scene. Now let us see what kind of disengagement was here being manifested. The persons themselves, if questioned, would have had no hesitation in saying that, so far from being disengaged, they were profoundly engaged in the community of scholarship and in the task of advancing knowledge.

The opposing point of view, which is often voiced by American politicians and was epitomized in the "Golden Fleece" awards of Senator Proxmire, is that those parts of the academic enterprise that are not engaged in teaching or in hard science or medicine are nothing other than a money-wasting sham. Academics, unlike politicians, misuse public resources for their private benefit. The motive imputed is that of economic individualism: people do whatever is in their own interest, whatever they might say about public service. The theory makes a very straightforward and familiar assumption about human nature: altruistic behavior in the public interest is not natural behavior. If unrestrained, people compete to help themselves. We are thus in the presence not only of most economists, but also of Plato, Machiavelli, Hobbes, Lenin, and all those many others who do not trust the common man and would take it as given that without limited entry the salmon in Alaska will be overfished, that without fences the common pastures will be grazed out of existence, and that without restrictive regulation groundwater in the San Joaquin valley will be polluted by chemical fertilizers and pesticides. Leviathan, not the collectivity but its ruler, not the people but the vanguard, must intervene. The academic pioneer in applying this theory to the provision of public goods wrote:

> In a large group in which no single individual's contribution makes a perceptible difference to the group as a whole, or the burden or benefit of any single member of the group, it is certain that a collective good will *not* be provided unless there is coercion or some outside inducements that will lead the members of the large group to act in their common interest. (Olson 1965:44, emphasis in original)

Olson does not talk about "human nature." He talks about what is "rational." But at the same time he seems to assume that his model is sufficiently close to reality to explain how people in trade unions or the American Medical Association or the American Association of University Professors conduct themselves, presumably because most of the time they are "rational." Strictly speaking, the theory makes no assumptions about human nature. It says no more than that *if* people are both rational and self-interested, they will fail to contribute voluntarily to the cost of public goods. The theory in itself does not assert that most people *are* rational and self-interested. But when it is used to explain why forests are overexploited and fisheries fished to extinction and ground water polluted by fertilizer runoff and university departments put into "administrative receivership" because the faculty is too lazy or too factious to manage its own affairs, then an assumption is being made about human nature. To be human, it is assumed, is to be rational and to be rational is to be self-interested, and that explains why people behave the way they do. The assumption then becomes a "fact of nature," a particular value for an independent variable that must be built into and therefore direct any kind of social engineering.

Does such a theory provide a fair portrait of the scholar dedicated to the study of Swahili poets or Tamil devotional literature? Are they freeloaders? Certainly they require the public goods of scholarship (notably a library or an archive) and, no less certainly, as individuals they make little or no contribution toward the provision and maintenance of the resources they use. Indeed sometimes they cheat by not performing the tasks which those who provide the public goods think they are paying for. They study poetry and devotional writing, when they are supposed to be training people in skills that have potential strategic value. Certainly also, as scholars with tunnel vision, they conform to the stereotype of rational choice insofar as they are largely indifferent to the possibility of cooperative endeavor. They are a type of scholar (as I remember them) that well deserves the adjective "individual," not only in a social sense but also intellectually, for they are more than a little wary of generalizing. If someone suggests that there may be a common framework that encompasses the structure of Tamil devotional literature and of Swahili poetry, they will exhibit, at most, a polite interest. They have very particular concerns, which cause them to be unsociable and unready to cooperate, if another scholar should dare venture into the field that they consider to be their own. That, by Olson's definition, is very "rational": the fear that your gain will be my loss, and the conviction that all resource games are zero-sum.[11] I recall also that similar "rational" zero-sum antipathies emerged over symbolic and quite petty things, such as the size of one's room in the university or the view from the window or whether one had a carpet on the floor.

But in other respects the portrait of the dedicated scholar as

---

[11]Some historians whom I knew at that time used to nail down a place and a period by announcing in print their intention to work in that field, perhaps with a short essay, or with an appeal for information about materials not in the public domain. In my own discipline, professors were usually careful to guide their research students away from topics or areas that "belonged" to a colleague, protecting the turf of both friends and rivals alike.

"economic man," maximizing his intellectual profits at the expense of other scholars, is fundamentally misdrawn. Certainly there could be, as I have indicated, territoriality over subject matter and a huge jealousy about reputations and honors. But those dedicated scholars did not habitually see themselves, in the manner of businessmen, as inevitable competitors for a single scarce resource. Quite the contrary: so long as people cultivated their own gardens, all would be well. They were not in a marketplace, competing for a limited fund of profit. Instead they were like gardeners growing flowers for their own delight, or like a miner who has found his own mother lode, a source of infinite riches to be gained without the help or the hindrance of others. Of course, reality for such persons is not like that: their self-contained world is a fantasy. Scholars need the library and the archives, the gardener needs seed catalogues, and the miner eventually needs a market for the gold. Even so, the scholarly image is truly one of a nonsocial individual, interacting less with other people than with things, whether the things be gold or flowers or *materia scholastica*.

Have we then found a presocial or nonsocial individual? I think not, and this will become clear if we move away from the fantasies of economic modeling to observed behavior.[12] When I recall those tunnel-visioned scholars and the context in which they worked and lived, it becomes quite difficult to sustain the picture of a presocial individualistic amorality, curmudgeons though they often were. To stay resolutely with the dogma that their behavior can be explained in the framework of undiluted individualism and rational action is to leave a great deal unexplained.

First, the choices and decisions, even of scholars, may not be

[12]*Fantasy* has, as one of its meanings, the way we would like the world to be. I use the word to indicate that formal modeling of purportedly natural systems of behavior is always to some extent prescriptive.

rational—that is, not consciously directed towards a particular end—but the product of habit or of unacknowledged psycho-dynamic forces. Second, as Russell Hardin demonstrated, rational choice theory rests on a "fallacy of static generalization," assuming that reasoning from rational behavior in "one-shot" situations (like the Prisoner's Dilemma, indeed a presocial situation) will continue to apply in repeated interactions between the same people (1982:3). In other words, people may learn to look to the future, to amend their choices, and in a perfectly rational fashion they may choose voluntarily to defer short-term personal advantage in return for the long-term benefits they get from collective action. Even the most inward-turned of scholars would leap to defend the ramparts, once they saw a threat to the autonomy of scholarly endeavor, even when it happened to be someone else's endeavor.[13] Third, as that last sentence indicates, choices, even when rational, are not *ipso facto* self-interested. To insist that they are is to beg the question. The "end" in a means-end calculation may be something other than the self. (Rational choice theorists, in other words, unduly limit the scope of rationality and beg a very large question at the outset.)[14] It seems clear that the dedicated scholars did in fact serve a collectivity of like-minded people, united by an ideology of autonomous scholarship and the advancement of knowledge. They were, to some degree, equipped with a sense of moral obligation toward a collectivity of people like themselves (not those who employed them), which more or less parallels the case of the workers on the shop floor who covered for each other.

[13]Ramparts were usually defended by inflicting one's presence on, or otherwise forcefully stating one's views to, the relevant committee; or by writing a strong letter to the London *Times* or the *Times Educational Supplement*.

[14]I draw these ideas from Robert Wade's *Village Republics* (1988), which has an excellent discussion of the economic basis for collective action.

PRACTICAL DISENGAGEMENT THROUGH THE USE OF VALUES

Certain possibilities for disengagement become available when it is not immediately clear whether duty or payment and punishment, consent or compliance, is the applicable mode. This disengagement is practical insofar as it exacts from the organization resources that it would prefer not to give. At the same time the means used are symbolic. A similar opportunism is possible when there appears to be a conflict of duties. The result might be called a practical version of flanneling. Ambiguity makes room for the disengager in the person of *tertius gaudens*.

Tertius gaudens, the "third man rejoicing," is one who profits from marginality. They are the people who exploit rivalries, pick up the spoils when the combatants have fought each other to a standstill, or, by playing off one party against another, preserve themselves from domination by either.[15]

We have many different words for people who are not centrally involved in an approved collectivity—outsider, loner, alien, foreigner, barbarian, upstart, intruder—all of which carry a greater or lesser hint of evil. If we do not suspect them, we pity them, thus assuming that normality is to belong and that marginality, if not ethically dubious, is at least unfortunate. Identities should be firmly anchored in a collectivity, not left ambiguous. That, obviously, is a norm advanced by institutions, since undivided loyalty to themselves is to their advantage. An individual who challenges an institution's demands on the grounds of higher duty cannot afford to do so crassly. The ice is particularly thin when one is near the edge, and as the dean's unfortunate young philosopher discovered, the higher

[15]Adas (1981:229–32) describes various ways in which Southeast Asian peasants protected themselves by playing off one master against another.

claims can be brushed off as shirking one's duty. The claim has to be made in such a way that the institution does not lose face.

There are two ways of making such a claim. One is straightforward and on the level of compliance rather than of consent: merely point out who is in control. The commanding institution is presented as all-powerful. Noncompliance will hurt not only the recusant individual but also the people who held him back. The department would be foolish not to release me for work that the dean or the chancellor badly wants me to do. Jury duty usually has this transcending power. In this situation there is some scope for disengagement; but not much, since such matters have little ambiguity in them.

The other situation calls for an adroit use of theater and it plays upon consent rather than compliance. The higher calling is presented as coming from a source that can in no way be a challenge to the institution's authority, because the institution subscribes to the same commanding value. Scholarship and the advancement of knowledge, as so far portrayed in this chapter, are exactly such values. Of course there is a threshold of scholarly distinction below which the claim is ineffective. But the institution that refuses to bend its rules for the distinguished individual pays a penalty of the loss of reputation when the scholar takes off for a more enlightened place where his talents are appreciated and where no one will bother if his committee service is nugatory and his teaching is lamentable.

How is such a reputation obtained? There are fields, for example in the natural sciences or mathematics, where major problems wait around to be solved, and the solver's name is instantly made. In other fields the "definitive study" or the "definitive edition" can work the same kind of magic. But matters are rarely so clear-cut, and even in these cases someone—a committee, reviewers, or some consenting body that carries weight—must agree that this is the correct solution or this is the definitive work. In other words reputation, recognition, and especially prizes (medals or election to elite associations) turn out to be political matters, matters of judgment and of opinion, of influence, lobbying, and other forms of pressure, matters as much involved with power as with truth. What you have discovered carries less weight than who can be persuaded to recognize you and your discovery, or, in many cases, as yet only your potential for discovery. The scholar is then less involved in a mute dialogue with an objective problem than in a noisy exchange with other scholars, who are collaborators or rivals. Such people are involved in networking, in getting invitations to conferences, in contributing to special issues of journals, in securing the right books for review or the right reviewers for their books, in winning grants for research, in acquiring patrons, in all the myriad undertakings that conceivably may advance them toward the solution of their intellectual problems, but certainly are not themselves intellectual endeavors. What starts out as honest dialectic, the search for truth by discussion, can easily become a bruising debate in which the adversaries are not solving problems but making or breaking reputations.

Those who play the market of reputations are not svejks, for svejks are not prima donnas; the role is always humble. Svejkism itself is their only virtuosity. Furthermore, as with Svejk himself, most of the time the authorities are anxious to see their backs and prefer to have them inflicting their eager presence elsewhere in the organization. Svejks can only operate, as *tertius gaudens*, on the level of the hierarchy's own proclaimed values. It is, as I said, a practical form of flanneling, in effect a form of blackmail, in which the organization's reputation for probity, its normative standing, would be threatened if the svejk's request were not granted.

The basic strategy is the use of a rhetoric that defines situations: *This situation is a type of . . ., variant of . . ., matter of . . ., the consequence of . . ., will be the cause of . . .*, and so forth. These definitions impose an asymmetry between what is actually known and what may effectively be brought to play to influence action. For example, once it is agreed that *This is a matter of principle*, then pragmatic justifications (*Think of the cost!*) are made invalid. Defining a proposed action as racist, in most of present-day America, forces actors to contest that definition before they can proceed to other justifications. A random dip into the gigantic thesaurus of contemporary constrainers produces *elitist, sexist, positivist, postmodernist, un-American, sub-university*, and, more generally, *matter of religion, . . . of conscience, . . . of principle, . . . of survival, unrealistic, prohibitive cost, suicidal*, and the like.

The situation is identified by means of a theatrical performance asserting the kind of person one is and inviting everyone concerned to join in the play, to collude. Moreover, there is always, beyond those invited to collude, a weightier potential audience; in other words, there is a threat to "go public." Such a move carries with it a message that both the svejks and their principals stand equally constrained by the higher verity, and at least in that respect are equal. Moreover, since the reminder has come from the svejk, it conveys an implicit claim to superior virtue and a suggestion that the principals are not as righteous as they might be. It is a tactic, as I said, that comes very close to flanneling.

Often these situations have been foreseen by the authorities, who then close off access to values that might be used for practical disengagement. I recall the mild envy we felt for the Jewish schoolboys among us. Certainly we did not envy them their faith.[16] What irritated was the fact that they had twenty minutes to finish last night's homework, while we were in the hall singing hymns and praying. They were disengagers who were,

[16]At that place and at that time (the 1930s) the normal attitude of the working classes was one of mild anti-Semitism, which did not go much beyond jokes about pawnbrokers, and was mostly disapproving of the antics of the Mosleyites.

compared to us, having it cushy. But it was also a situation without further tactical possibilities. Religion's impingement on school routines had long since been defined by the city's education department. The same is true in my recollection of the army and of various universities; there was little scope for opportunistic redefinition of the boundary between duty to the organization and religious or family obligation or whatever else.

There was more scope for opportunistic redefinition of the situation by fastening, theatrically, on the organization's shortcomings. Given the vast facade of pretense that fronts any organization—that it behaves rationally, that all do their duty and are concerned with the general interest and not with particular interests, that the institution is like a good parent toward its members, and so forth—there are inevitably veins of hypocrisy to be mined by would-be disengagers. The situation calls for finesse, because any well-established institution has a vast fail-safe apparatus designed exactly to prevent its shortcomings from being noticed, or, if noticed, from being used against it. The would-be svejk is then faced not with defining a situation that was hitherto unnoticed (simply blowing the whistle), but with discrediting the label that the institution has already placed on the situation by means of all those devotion-creating poetics described earlier.

Moreover (with an exception to be noted shortly) whistle-blowing is rarely the way of a svejk. Anyone who goes public with his complaints about institutional shortcomings, *with the intention of doing something to correct them*, is an activist, not a svejk. The prudent svejk cuts himself into the deal and trades silence about the action for a piece of it. The exchanges are realistic, premised upon how the organization actually works, not how it should work, or how officials pretend it works. Svejk's performative definition of himself—a worldly-wise sensible person who knows his best interests and who can be trusted, if properly rewarded, not to rock the boat—matches

the institution's pragmatism. His poetics do not appeal upward
to transcending values and higher loyalties of the hierarchical
kind, but point pragmatically downward toward narrower interests. Again the situation resembles that which makes flanneling possible: authorities are hamstrung by their own regulations. The difference, of course, is that svejk as a flanneler
challenges authority by mocking higher values. In the present
case svejks make no challenge. They just quietly take their
profit.

There remains one other way in which a svejk can disengage
by identifying himself with higher values. As before, the institution is identified with its own shortcomings, but this time in
the mode of a public statement. This is the svejkism practised
by a Bad University Man, who does not directly elevate his
own image, but instead degrades that of the institution. Useful
rhetorical constrainers are *time-wasting, busy-work, paperwork,
obsessed with trivia.* Behind it all is a vast folklore that condemns
all administrators as failed scholars and thinkers (or even failed
teachers); anyone eager to perform institutional duties, it is implied, has lost sight of the higher values of learning. It follows,
in this simple rhetorical non sequitur, that those who noisily
despise committee work and administration must therefore be
involved with scholarship. The tactic resembles the use of networking to give the appearance of scholarly distinction, when
there is no substance.

The message can be conveyed in a performance without
words, as in the case of those scholars, described earlier, who
absented themselves the first days of the term in case they
might be obliged to take on a student. Incompetence at committee work can also help, but an active Svejk-like capacity to
create chaos while maintaining a posture of innocent enthusiasm is even better. Of course, in some cases this is not a posture at all, but the real person. I have a vivid recollection of a
five-person committee, met to give advice on a colleague's promotion, and chaired by a scholar who combined vast distinc-

tion with small common sense. Such committees usually meet once. On this occasion they had four meetings (one member protesting that there was not enough Valium in the world to get her to a fifth encounter with that chairman) and produced a flush of five minority reports. The message taken, intended or not, was very clear: that particular chairman should be left to get on with his research.

A reputation for eager administrative incompetence can stand alone, even when not bracketed with the higher values of scholarship, as an effective protector of individual space. But it does not work the same way in all organizations. In academia there is no formal punishment for being bad at committees, because in such self-governing institutions members are requested and not ordered to do such work. Armies are not governed by committee and soldiers are expected to carry out efficiently the tasks given them. Nor can Svejk work the rhetorical side of the street, as a scholar can, by claiming that everyday incompetence goes along with distinction in higher fields. Underlying these differences is the fact that universities recognize the institution's need for illustrious individuals, whose presence lends it glory. Armies try not to do so (but, as the next chapter shows, cannot in fact operate without some level of individual autonomy).

Any institution faces a hazard from the fact that it exists in a context of other institutions and of values that may transcend or encompass its own values. Individuals have an opportunity to refuse service to the institution on the grounds of a higher calling. Most institutions protect themselves beforehand against members' claims to be serving higher values by specifying precisely how far such a calling will be allowed to interfere with obligations to the institution. Even when the limits are not precisely stated because the institution is built around the accomplishments of individual members, institutional service is apt to be taken as the norm and visible disengagement requires theatrically marked justification. which can be done in several ways. One is the direct invocation of higher ends, as in the case of the networking scholar. Another, less direct, is to denounce the institution as itself failing to observe proper values. This tactic is used by scholars who say committees are a waste of time and they themselves have better things to do. Yet more indirect is the original svejk who professes enthusiasm but displays only incompetence. Finally, there is the garden variety of svejkism in which institutional shortcomings are quietly recognized and cannily exploited.

ECONOMIC INDIVIDUALISM

Practical disengagement is the covert appropriation by individuals of resources that the organization would prefer not to have given. The standard model for understanding that kind of behavior is economic individualism. The model is intellectually docile, a well-trained dog. It does not drag the investigator off the smooth path of rationality, which is pointed toward quantification, into the thorny scrub where people act out of spite or moral outrage or self-respect or for the love of God or, most annoying of all, just for the fun of it.

The model seems to have much to commend it. First it lays bare the essential hypocrisy of holism, by showing who benefits. Those who have power in an organization have a clear interest in sacralizing it, in making its service primarily a matter of conscience and duty. Holism stabilizes their command and helps to keep them feeling good about themselves; when they punish people, they can claim to be acting for the good of all, including the offenders. Holism provides a convenient rhetoric from behind which to exercise power.

Economic individualism also seems to be a handy philosophy for both principals and agents. It teaches the principals that every man has his price and can be bought, by reward or penalty. The way to stop workers from cheating on the time sheets or ruining the cutting heads or any other kind of shirking is to make it not worth their while to do so. Workers are like machines: if properly adjusted, they work properly. It may be the case that workers, unlike machines, have feelings, but those feelings can be tuned out of any transaction by suitable reward or punishment. The hierarchy that encompasses Jesus and his disciples is really a contract between them. It has nothing to do with miracles; the disciples, like everyone else, just come for the loaves and the fishes. Moreover, even if they really did come for the miracles or for the love of God, that fact can be tuned out and ease of quantification restored, as soon as one realizes that mind-sets appreciating miracles and loving God are essentially the product of management policy and management investment. Military mind-sets likewise are the product of time and energy invested in brainwashing procedures. Brainwashing can be subjected to cost-benefit analysis; there is no need to get inside anyone's head and find out about their feelings, when their actual behavior can be observed and measured.[17]

The model also teaches the disengagers what to do. It teaches them that the organizational world is a zero-sum world and the measure of the organization's loss is their gain. A decision to disengage is a rational calculation of the benefit to be got from cheating against the chances and the costs of being caught and punished; right and wrong have no part in the calculation. That kind of rationality informs the peasants who cheat the agents who come to collect the tithe; they expect to get away with it. Workers fiddle the time-categories so that

---

[17]Black box models, which statistically connect input with output without otherwise explaining the connection, are inherently less useful than models that take the black box to pieces and show *how* cause and consequence are connected.

they can get more money for their work than management wants to give them.

But, throughout this chapter, as soon as that rational cost-benefit model has been shown to fit the case, conduct comes to light that is not encompassed by the model. It seems that to be practical about shirking, sooner or later disengagers must let themselves be moved by ideas of duty and loyalty. Peasants cooperate with other peasants, and workers with their fellows on the shop floor, and on occasions with the officials who are supposed to be monitoring them, even when no immediate payoff is apparent. Sometimes, of course, it is a matter of enlightened self-interest. Those who do not cooperate get sent to Coventry or worse. But is that always the case? If it is, then morality must be more narrowly distributed than our experiences commonly tell us. The quite reflexive knowledge of solidarity that workers on occasions attest to must be an illusion. So also must be a kind of action that is within everyone's experience: people sometimes do what they see as intrinsically right, even at their own cost.

Even more difficult for the rational self-interest framework is conduct that is patently not rational in any material sense. "Homers" or flanneling or the idiocies of carnival and the Companies of Fools can be construed as utility functions. So also can maximizing personal dignity, self-respect, defiance, bloody-mindedness, or whatever else. The same is true even for things that just make a person feel good—the problem solved or the definitive work of scholarship that is experienced as rewarding even when there has been no external certification. But what is the point of construing them that way, when no one knows how to quantify such variables and build them into a formula that will predict behavior?

But there is a problem more fundamental than measurement alone. Economic individualism does not sufficiently concern itself with *personal dignity*, with the sense that we have of our own existence, separate and apart from the collectivities that contain us. Those qualities and experiences—a sense of achievement, bloody-mindedness, self-respect, doing things for the fun of it, above all the sense of personal dignity—are not understood but simply pushed out of sight when they are crammed into the mode of contract.

Chapter 5

Personal Dignity

Let us thank God for valour in abstraction
For those who go their own way. . . .
　　　　　—Louis MacNeice,
　　　　　　　"Eclogue from Iceland"

THE RATIONAL SCHOOLBOY

The normal time in Six Alpha, the classical sixth form, was three years, and some of the teaching, I have since come to realize, was quite uninspired, especially in the lower "bench" (middle and upper were better). The school was cramming us to compete for a scholarship to Oxford or Cambridge (no point in doing classics anywhere else, they told us). We were being trained essentially to be intellectual technicians, skilled at construing a sentence in Greek or Latin, recognizing, or even composing in, the various meters, dactylic, iambic, spondaic, or trochaic, and able to describe in summary fashion the reforms of Cleisthenes or the campaigns of the Punic Wars. But in that first year especially, and even in later years, a lot more was said about the technicalities of language than about content. What content remained was meager, and the larger patterns of ideas, where some real intellectual pleasures are to be found, were left to fend for themselves. So was much else: it was not until I went to Oxford and heard Gilbert Murray read aloud an extended passage from Euripedes, that I realized how much this was poetry, how there could be music in the sounds.

In history, during that first sixth-form year, we worked from a textbook that appended to each chapter a summary in note form. At the end of the week in which the master had finished his discussion of a chapter (mostly a paraphrase with lengthy quotes and advice as to what was important enough to be memorized), he administered a written test. We knew when these tests were coming and most of us prepared for them by making, in microscopic handwriting on a card, a crib of what we thought mattered in the notes. No one was ever caught; marks were good (we did take care to make an occasional mistake to lend plausibility to our excellence); it was a satisfactory arrangement (albeit fraudulent) for all concerned.

We also had a weekly exercise at written "unseen" translation from the Greek. The master used a set of battered texts, which contained excerpts from various authors. Each week he wrote on the blackboard the page and lines to be translated. But the texts had been in use many years, always with the same passages examined, and apparently always in the same order, so that one had no difficulty in looking surreptitiously ahead and finding the slight pencil marks around the passage that would come next week. Then one could get a copy of the relevant author from the library, and use Liddell and Scott's lexicon to prevent the examination from in fact being "unseen." (Occasionally we found a Loeb text, which has a translation on the facing page; but using this was considered to be perilously near real cheating.) The master must have known what was going on. He may have been too lazy to change his ways; or he may have reckoned that the effort of tracking down the passage and using the lexicon was in itself sufficient training; at least we had the incentive to look up the words beforehand, rather than neglect to do so afterwards.

These are mild instances of svejkism. We broke the rules; we were not punished; the operations paid off in the form of good marks. Not everyone survived into the upper sixth, but those who did worked hard, mixing, in an odd way, the kind of devotion to the task that signals legitimacy for the institution, with a measure of low-key, but quite unmistakable, and some-times cynical, detachment, exemplified in the cheating that I have just described.

These small examples set the question that shapes the rest of this chapter. What is the experience that gives one a sense of being an individual? What conditions go along with the exer-cise of individual initiatives? Why is it that the performances intended to manufacture devotion, those investments in mem-ber-mindlessness, are never totally effective and sometimes quite ineffective? The answers considered—there are others in the psychodynamic domain, with which I am not here con-cerned—revolve around the task that the organization is ex-pected to perform and the way this task affects individual expe-rience.

Why did we cheat? One answer is obvious. We could appear to do what the organization demanded that we do, without running the risk of failing a test. Clearly the school was power-ful. No one dreamt of refusing to take the tests; open defiance would have meant real trouble. Neither did anyone want the lesser trouble of a test badly done. But at the same time the tests themselves were not granted legitimacy; we saw nothing sacred in them, and were not in the least captured by that strange sense of awe and challenge, experienced later when we went up to Oxford or Cambridge to sit scholarship examina-tions. I think now that making a crib and preparing a vocabu-lary beforehand to cope with the unseen exams were effective learning devices; but at the time it seemed no more than a matter of saving oneself trouble. We were giving the organiza-tion the form it wanted (an examination), without the sub-stance; and for ourselves we were doing exactly the opposite, getting the substance (knowledge), without having to go through the tedious and slightly perilous performances (real tests) that the organization demanded.

Why were we allowed to cheat in this discreet fashion (assuming I am right in thinking the masters knew what was going on)? The school, as I said, did reasonably well in the fierce competition for Oxbridge scholarships. That success partly reflects the teaching, which was not all of the kind I have just described. It also reflects a very strong agreement between the sixth-form pupils and the school itself about the nature of the school's task. Efficiency was measured by academic success. Getting to a university—if not Oxbridge, then the city's own university—was the be-all and end-all of sixth-form life. Those who survived into the sixth form had the kind of ambition that characterized many families in the lower middle class; to "better" oneself was the phrase our parents used. The headmaster and the sixth-form masters had matching ambitions: to reproduce themselves in pupils who, as they had done, would gain university degrees.

REFLEXIVE INDIVIDUALISM

The school, as I look back on it, was an extraordinarily competitive place. The boys were constantly involved in something that had victory as its goal. Teams from the different houses, organized by age, competed at soccer and at cricket (not enough boys played rugby or field hockey to make league competition between houses possible).[1] There was a league table and at the end of the season one team was at the top, and the rest, in order of merit, were below it. The school competed with other secondary schools in the same way, at all four

[1]The working classes followed soccer and cricket. In that region (but not everywhere in Britain) amateur rugby was mostly a middle-class game, and field hockey (which can be no less brutal that soccer or rugby) was considered a girl's game.

sports. About half the time of each twice-weekly hour in the gymnasium was spent in competitive encounters of one sort or another, mostly between teams picked for the occasion. Most of the sports were team sports: no golf, no tennis, fistfights enough but no organized boxing. The exceptions were field sports, running races and jumping and the like, and swimming; the competitors in those were individuals. But even there, for example in cross-country running, success was measured as much by team placement as by individual performance. Of course there were sports "heroes," and the captains of the several school teams were prestigious individuals. Nevertheless, competitive sports focused as much on cooperation as on competition, and were, for the most part, holistic in the message they delivered.

Academic competition, so far as I remember, was entirely individualistic. I can remember nothing that was ever done in teams. In the third, fourth, and fifth forms (at least in the upper streams) lessons consisted partly of question and answer. The term began with the boys seated in alphabetical order by surname. The master asked the boy in the first place a question, which, if he failed to answer correctly, was passed on to the next boy, and so on down the line until someone got it right. The winner then moved up to sit where the first loser had sat, and all the losers moved down a place. The next question went to the boy next below the last of the losers. I do not remember that this game caused the chaos that it sounds like it should have done. I do remember that to stay near the top one had to be alert, and only those down at the bottom were given to dozing (until the master decided to liven them up by breaking the pattern and firing a question at someone down their end of the class). Misbehavior, such as "talking in class" or blatant daydreaming, could also result in being "sent down bottom."

Whether the results of this daily exercise in academic elbowmanship ever got into the final ranking, I do not know.

There were constant tests, and an examination at the end of each term, and the boys were ranked by academic merit. Top and second place of each form at the end of the year were marked by an award (always books) at the annual prize-giving, a grand affair at which a distinguished person (for example, the city's lord mayor or a member of Parliament) gave the prizes and made a speech that customarily had two features that were cherished by the boys because, we naively believed, they upset the headmaster: a request for an extra half-holiday for us, and the heretical claim that he, the great man, had never himself won a prize at school.

At the age of nine one could compete for a junior city scholarship, success being marked by a certificate and a grant to pay the annual school fees (equivalent to about what a skilled worker would earn in four weeks). At about twelve, if in the high stream, one entered for matriculation, and if that was passed at a high enough level, one began to prepare for the higher school certificate examination and the serious competition for senior city scholarships that took one to the local university, for state scholarships (a national competition, and armed with which one could usually get entrance into an Oxford or Cambridge college) and, most prestigious of all, open scholarships or (ranked lower) exhibitions given by Oxford or Cambridge colleges.

There were, logically enough, no *collective* rituals to celebrate competition between individuals as a central feature in the life of the school, until the moment of success, when one's name appeared in the lists published by the national and local newspapers, and the triumphs were prominently featured in the headmaster's address at the prize-giving. Theatrical encouragement in the shape of collective cultural performances would anyway have been redundant, like rain-magic in Cherrapunji. We had the ethic of personal success already, and needed no further enchantment in that direction. Competition was practical, everyday and individualistic, like the game of musical chairs up and down the form, and the neverending testing and examining. The only theater that I recall, apart from the once-yearly award of prizes, was an inversion: the standardized ridicule visited on the studious by those in the lower streams, the epithet "swot."

I do not know how typical this school was of all those in England that carried education beyond the age of sixteen. I suspect schools like it were to be found in other industrial cities that were then (1930s) in a process of decay. The hunger for achievement was at least in part connected with socioeconomic class. No one in that school could at that time have gone to Oxford or Cambridge by any other than the scholarship route. No one had family connections with a college, and no families were wealthy enough to afford tertiary education for their sons. We were, of course, beating a system, the class system; but we rarely thought of the struggle in those terms.[2] Our parents used the phrase "bettering oneself." To better oneself, when one's father was an unskilled laborer, was to have a trade, which is to have been apprenticed and be a journeyman, a skilled worker. We were going one better, moving beyond trades into the professions.

Nor was it simply a matter of money, although that was important. "Trade" in the other sense—anything from shopkeeper to bookmaker—was ambivalently viewed, with envy if the person was prosperous, but with a frequently voiced suspicion that people in trade could not be entirely honest. Also there was risk; a business was always a bit of a gamble. But a profession was different: honest, "doing good," and secure. That was how our parents viewed doctors, clergymen, and even schoolteachers (lawyers were too remote, and I do not

[2]That came later, usually after we had in fact beaten the system, got to the university, and become bourgeois in our ambitions and our life-styles, if not yet in our incomes. Then at last, having left it, we showed solidarity with the working class, by joining one of the university's left-wing political clubs.

recall them being mentioned). Above all, it was generally assumed that in the professions there were no foremen and no bosses; you could be your own person. This is the naive Protestantism—work hard and get ahead of the others and keep your hands clean (in both senses of that phrase)—that shaped our attitude toward academic success. We, as sons of the working class, constituted a hopeless case of false consciousness, mostly unaware of our proletarian interests and on the verge of losing our proletarian identity.

We learned to be individuals in two distinct ways, which came one after the other. "Bettering oneself," it was assumed, was *not* a collective thing. (This segment of the working class was extremely ambivalent about unions, and many of them voted Conservative.) People were arranged in a pyramid, and there was always less room higher up than down below. You were on your own, you were a competitor, you did not want to lose; you made your own place in the world. So you were an individual against other individuals.

But later, even as early as the lower sixth form and certainly by the time one went to university, the view began to change. The opponent now was less other individuals, who had to be beaten into second place, and more the tasks that had to be done, problems to be solved, patterns to be perceived where they had not been seen before. You were bettering yourself still, but in a different way; not by defeating others but by the solitary exercise of a creative intellect, by cogitation. This is a turning inward, finding one's identity through contact with things (ideas and problems and patterns) rather than with people or against people. This is reflexive individualism; an experience of the self that is not mirrored in the eyes of other people. Competition, beating the other person, may be antisocial, but it is at the same time certainly social in the sense that it must involve interaction with other people. To call it individualism is common enough and not a misuse of the word, but it mostly means that the speaker disapproves of the competitor's self-interested motives. The other kind of individualism, although obviously dependent on social and cultural facilities (books, schools, even debate and conversation) is effectively nonsocial. That, in the end, was the individualism for which the school trained us; they wanted to make us the individual of *cogito ergo sum*. In this way the intellect becomes the foe of any collectivity, because a collectivity calls for true-belief, not cogitation.

Schools and colleges and tertiary education were not the only places where the individualism of *cogito ergo sum* was to be found. Take the case of my uncle George.

THE SELF-MADE MAN

George Tyler was a pattern-maker, working in a ship yard on Merseyside. A pattern-maker fashioned in wood a form (pattern) which was used to make a mold for metal castings of complicated and exact things like cogwheels for marine engines. It was a very highly skilled trade. When he was in his late twenties his wife received a legacy and they used it to open a restaurant in a seaside resort. When he was thirty-five, they retired, having made and invested enough money to support themselves in modest leisure for the rest of their lives. They lived in six or seven places, successively, always in the country. In a few places they ran a small catering business, but most of their time was spent improving the house and the garden where they lived. Then, after four or five years, they would buy or build another house in another place and begin the cycle of improvement again.

Uncle George was not simply self-made; he was also self-educated. He taught himself to read music and bought a pedal organ. Although a town dweller by origin, he acquired a considerable knowledge of natural history, all of it from books and encyclopedias. He had a fine garden and grew exotic flowering shrubs, varieties that his neighbors had never seen. He kept bees and chickens and rabbits and sold the surplus produce. He exhibited things he made, in particular wooden bowls of an intricate layered design, and won prizes at the county fair. Much of this knowledge was its own delight; much also was put to practical use. He knew not only about woodworking, but also about engines and electricity and plumbing and radio and roofing and bricklaying and sewers and the weather and the stars and the clouds. A slight and frail man, weakened by severe surgery in his early forties, he nevertheless undertook tasks that would have been far too strenuous, had he not devised various mechanical contrivances to make nature do the work. He lived, so to speak, by the principle of the lever. He had a liking for gadgets of all kinds, providing they were useful, and took particular delight when he found one that he could take apart and remake to a more efficient design. Life for him, I suspect, was best when it presented a rich continuance of problems, practical and intellectual, to be faced and solved.

In his own way he was a creature of the Enlightenment. I do not mean that such people did not exist before the eighteenth century; I mean that he conformed perfectly to its standards—rational, skeptical, with a passion for learning and a thorough contempt for mysticism of any kind. He and his wife attended the village church and played their part in collective village enterprises—the annual fete and the Women's Institute and the like—but he did so in anything but the spirit of *noblesse oblige*; rather he saw it in the mode of a village Hobbes—it was the rational and ultimately self-interested thing to do. In the same vein, he concealed his total contempt for the local squire and for the squirearchy in general (I am thinking of one particular place in Dorset where he lived for about seven years), because to have behaved otherwise would have been a counterproductive symbolic gesture. There was nothing to be gained by silly behavior. There was never anything to be gained by losing control over one's feelings. He had, in any case, a marked dislike for gestures and symbolic acts and for anything that he considered just words—that is, for rhetoric. The people worthy of his respect were the people who did things.

He considered the squire—a retired naval officer, with a hyphenated name, who always used his former rank as a title—to be an ineffectual empty-headed man who had never worked for his living, and who had not earned his wealth, only inherited some and married the rest. For the same reason both he and his wife had an equally staunch disapproval of the unemployed. This was in the 1930s, during the depression. A feature in *Picture Post*, describing the miseries of living on the dole, aroused their especial contempt. The man was obviously lazy and without spirit; and the woman must be a stupid and improvident housekeeper not to be able to make do on that amount of money. With that attitude, and being himself essentially now a *rentier*, he supported the Tory party, without, however, having much respect for its leaders.

Uncle George thought of himself as a decent civic-minded person, and would have indignantly rejected a suggestion that his rational individualism and his somewhat skeptical attitude toward collectivities made him a free rider. Already an elderly man when the war came, he volunteered to work unpaid as a stoker in the boiler room of a hospital in the county town (characteristically getting books from the library to make sure he understood that particular heating system). Equally characteristically, he stayed with the work until one day the matron publicly rebuked him for refusing to perform some menial task that had nothing to do with the boilers; then he gave her a piece of his mind and quit. He believed in "pulling his weight." He did not believe in letting others get away without doing their share or get more than they deserved, and, other than in obvious cases of sickness and disability, he considered failure mostly a voluntary matter and therefore blameworthy.

Quite consistently, when he served a collectivity, he did so in a spirit of enlightened self-interest. Associations existed for a purpose, not as ends in themselves. Talk of "community" (in the sense of *Gemeinschaft*) he would have bracketed away as nonsense designed as a cover for those too lazy or too stupid to make their own way in life. A community was as irrational and as irresponsible as a mob. I think he would have had a similarly dismissive opinion of the unconscious, but I do not know whether his reading ever went in that direction.

In the person of my uncle George, we arrive at the real (and, at least in his case, victorious) enemy of holism. Uncle George certainly had a philosophy, which he could articulate clearly. One's fate was mostly in one's own hands; one had a mind that should be exercised in solving problems; success was making enough money to live as one wished; the good life was one spent in devising solutions for problems; and, very important, one should be one's own master, because chances were that a boss would be relatively stupid (as the matron proved to be). The philosophy is not that of Calvinism and Weber's protestant ethic, because it has no place for God and for salvation. It is a form of liberal rationalism, positivist in outlook and accepting social responsibility to the extent that it is expedient to do so.

Uncle George flourished in the relatively laissez-faire capitalist ambience that characterized Britain between the wars. But that environment is only one example of the type of social structure that calls for Uncle George's design for living. Now I shall look at that same mentality, the mind made individual by problem-solving, as the (unlikely) product of certain forms of military training.

THE CONTEXTS OF INDIVIDUALISM

The sergeant, who amused himself in the middle of a war by teaching us the drill used when a royal cortege passes by on its way to Westminster Abbey—rifle-muzzle on the toe-cap of the left boot, hands folded over the stock, body erect but head inclined downward—ended his instruction with the command "Look sad, you buggers!" There was no suggestion that we should *feel* sad, only that we should wear the mask that was appropriate to the occasion.

But sometimes a mask is not what the organization wants; it wants the real thing. About the same time that we learned what to do with a rifle at a funeral, we were also being put through other more practical drills. One was the use of a bayonet on a straw and hessian life-size victim, which was sometimes erect in a frame and other times lay flat on the ground. One plunged the whole twelve inches of the bayonet in, then put a boot on the victim so that one could grasp the rifle near the muzzle and pull the bayonet out of the body. The instructor explained that in a real body the bayonet could get stuck between the bones, and that was why you had to use your boot. Recruits with a vivid imagination and a weak stomach found this exercise unsettling. Furthermore, when one thrust the bayonet in, one was required to make a loud noise that indicated a combination of exultation and hatred. This demonstration was not intended to be a mere show of emotion, as in "Look sad, you buggers!" The idea was that the adrenalin should flow and one should really feel exultation and hatred.

The army in fact went to all kinds of lengths to manipulate emotions and around them to reshape the recruit's personality. The theory, a commonsense one, was that if you act out an emotion often enough, you will feel it. Or if you act out its suppression often enough, it will be suppressed. Cultural performances, pretense, permit skepticism only among those who manage to remember that they are *performances*. But if the performances are well done, and frequently done, they cease to be performances and achieve some kind of reality of their own. This reality is a modification in the personality of the trainee.

Emotions like hatred and anger and any feelings that arouse competitiveness and move one to spontaneous unthinking action were considered positive. The army also took care of emotions that inhibit action; in particular it took care of fear. Our instructors were fixated on heights. They slung ropes between tall trees, preferably over an expanse of water, and the trainees had to swarm along them; they set a four-inch beam fifteen feet above ground, and made the recruit walk along it, carrying a rifle and with a pack on his back, which made him top-heavy and likely to overbalance. The instructors were not at all put out by the physical distress caused by heights in some people. Willpower was supposed to conquer phobias, and an unfortunate victim had to vomit or faint before the pressure was taken off. (This was an officer-training unit for armored troops, and failure to master a fear of heights could mean a return to the ranks. One wonders how many talented tank commanders were wasted that way.) In one part of the obstacle course the trainee ran full-tilt up a sandy slope toward a cliff, while an instructor screamed at him to go faster and threw a thunder-flash (a large firecracker) behind him. Then, suddenly, just as the instructor screamed "Jump!" the whole of Surrey stretched itself out panoramically, seeming hundreds of feet below. Indeed a leap into the unknown, a jump into the bottomless abyss, into infinity! In fact there was little danger, because one fell no more than twelve or fifteen feet and rolled down a slope of soft sand; but it was unnerving. Later, the climax of the course, we went to the mountains of north Wales and did the same kinds of exercise while the instructors fired live ammunition around us. Only one person from our squad was lost to the army, a Canadian volunteer who was hit in the lung by a bullet ricocheting from the surface of a lake.

In some ways this exercise is like drill-square indoctrination; it is designed to change the personality. To some extent also, it is a change in the direction of mindlessness, in a very literal sense. Fear and hesitation, normal prudence and forethought are suspended, and one discovers that the body and its sensitivities can be punished to an extent that formerly would have been unthinkable. Such training, as they said accurately enough, made a new man of you.

But in other ways this induction into the extremes of physical and emotional stress was quite unlike the perfectly coordinated symmetrical performances of the parade ground. Battle drills did, of course, require coordinated movement; that was partly the point of the training. But the obstacle courses, the extreme measures taken to make adrenalin flow and funnel it toward the appropriate emotion and action, and the consistent effort to reshape the personality, were all directed at the individual, not so as to make him faceless (as in parade-ground drills) but to give him a sense of being in charge of himself and in control of his body and his feelings. The "new man" thus made could conquer fatigue and fear. The training, moreover, taught defiance. It pitted the individual against the instructor. A common reaction to the screaming injunction to try harder was momentary hatred, followed by the thought "I'll show the bastard! I can do it!" Notice that this is "I," not the "we" of the drill squad. It also pitted the new man against himself, against his own body and his own instincts. *Excrucior, ergo sum,*[3] some trainee Descartes might have said. It was a highly personal, highly individual experience; it gave one self-confidence, that stubborn inner strength that is the beginning of being ungovernable. The new man, in other words, was not at all holistic man. The modern drill square mostly serves the end of collective dignity; this other kind of training is mostly to do with the individual's efficiency. Its effect was to invest individuals with a personal reflexive dignity, with a consciousness of and a respect for their own agonistic selves.

The point can be made in another way. There was a time when the maneuvers learned on the drill square were also the maneuvers employed in battle. Mindless choreographed movement and mindlessness itself, in the appropriate circumstances, also serve the end of efficiency. The circumstances are usually those which require a demonstration of massive, impersonal, and unrelenting force. The phalanx of the Greek armies was a

[3] I am in pain, therefore I am.

line of battle composed of heavy infantry (hoplites) armed with long spears. By the time of Alexander the phalanx was no less than sixteen men deep, and its strength depended upon the soldiers standing firm. Individual initiatives, whether running ahead or running away, are makers of disaster because they break the line. In other words, there are situations in which both institutional dignity and institutional efficiency are directly served by coordinated movement. The phalanx was no doubt impressive, in the way that any large body of men, moving in a disciplined fashion, is impressive; and it was effective, given the weapons of the day. But it called for no more initiative from the individual soldier than was needed to step forward and take the place of the man in front, if he fell in the battle.

Cavalry charges notionally have a similar quality; they should work best if every trooper makes contact with the enemy at the same time. But at that point the line dissolves into individualized combat, with a lance or a sword. Then it pays to do the unexpected. Mikhail Sholokov's Cossack hero in the *Don* trilogy could use his sabre equally effectively with either hand. Singling out his enemy, a few yards short of contact, he would switch sword hands and so guide his horse that he attacked from the side away from the opponent's sword-arm. That is the model for a soldier trained in the mode of the obstacle course, trained to think that survival and winning the fight depend upon how determined and how skilful and adroit and how quick and how cunning he is himself. In the 1939–45 army I recall one exercise in particular that brought home the lesson of self-reliance. Trainees were taken by night in a truck thirty miles away and dumped, one by one, without money or food or maps, and told to find their own way back to camp.[4]

---

[4]This was not a simple test of physical endurance; ingenuity counted, and there were no penalties for the soldier smart enough to talk himself into a free bus ride.

Armies, for reasons that are easily understood, are ambivalent about individualized initiatives. The cavalry charge, at the moment of impact, is a maker of disarray and the force that can bring itself back to order is the force likely to prevail. The Cavaliers paid that price. "Prince Rupert's horse charged once, often with devastating effect, but then lost cohesion in the search for plunder and destroying enemy stragglers. . . . [They] could not be brought to make a second charge the same day." Cromwell's cavalry, even if beaten, rallied and in that way their repeated charges at Marston Moor turned a likely defeat into a victory (Hill 1988:76–77).

The point, more precisely made, is that in the Second World War, although there were set-piece battles in plenty, with artillery barrages and tanks, and calling for phalanxlike qualities from the infantrymen (Alamein comes to mind), and although then, as in every other war, no battles were won by an undisciplined rabble, there was also a war of movement demanding the constant exercise of individual initiatives and requiring the kind of person who can exit from the mentality of a collectivity and think for himself. Efficiency of this kind requires individualism, the capacity to act when there are no rules, and sometimes in defiance of the rules. Circumstances are in their detail unpredictable, and training is designed to produce a predictable reaction to unpredictability—don't panic and use your head. Regulation by the organization is thus rendered more general, less specific, and more open to interpretation by intelligent individuals.

This requirement does not, of course, negate loyalty to the collectivity and its values. Such a person can sacrifice himself no less than the mindlessly regimented person. The individual is not necessarily *self*-interested; he may be, but that is not the point. The point is, first, that he is sufficiently detached to be able to look critically at the means the organization wants him to use, and second, that the situation is often such that the organization has not been able to tell him what means to use.

Third, means and ends are not always that easy in practice to keep separate, so that the ends too can come into question. Commando training did not produce mutineers; but neither did it produce robots. It fostered a critical detached intelligence, trained to work out the best way of getting a particular job done, the job always expected to have in it an element of the unexpected. Soldiers of that kind do not see themselves as cannon fodder, but as specialists, as experts.

Not unexpectedly in units trained in this way the immense interactive distance between officers and other ranks, caricatured in Svejk's army, was much diminished. Even in more conventional units, including the Brigade of Guards, which lay at the feudal end of the British class structure, the combination of danger, of dealing with the unexpected, of expertise, and of small groups, could foster a similar intelligent individualism.

EXPERTISE

The category of citizen soldiers least amenable to theater-induced mindless consent, to the suppression of personal dignity, came from urban industrial backgrounds. Why were they resistant?

The readiest explanation is that they were unionized in civil life, were socialist in outlook, and were therefore what, at that time, army officers and the managerial class in general called "bolshie." There is something in this analysis; although not much for the soldiers I knew. True, some of them had heard of false consciousness and the coming proletarian revolution, and there was even an enthusiast. I recall him joyfully waving a copy of the *Daily Worker* at some rather wary Russian soldiers, when the armies met in the middle of Germany. But there were no others like him in the unit, and he was treated, with some indulgence, as an amiable crank. In any case, even if party members had been numerous, to be "bolshie" is not to be resistant to collectivism; it is only to give one's loyalty to a different collectivity.

The self-respect that I remember as a feature of these troopers in fact had little to do with class solidarity. They were somewhat mixed; most were from the working class or the lower middle class but a proportion came from occupations or from families (many were too young to have had a job before enlistment) that were characteristically bourgeois: white-collar people. The self-respect had more to do with a way of perceiving the social world that is characteristic of industrial societies: it is a kind of atomization, of fragmentation, particularizing, a readiness to see oneself as distinct from others. This, of course, is the individualism that emerged in the eighteenth century. But the troopers were not philosophers, and knew nothing of the Enlightenment, and derived their ideas directly from socialization and experience, especially the experience of work and of schooling.

The evolutionary model set out earlier links the emergence of industrial society with increased exchange, which in turn is linked with specialization. Peasants are not specialized; each peasant has many different skills. In industrial societies the scope of specialization is vastly enlarged and is one reason for their greater productivity. It also provides each worker with a personal domain from which both bosses and other workers are at least partially excluded. To make this clear the concept *worker* must be dismantled.

Seen from the distant perspective of political economy, the grim streets around Britain's dark satanic mills—or the working class suburbs that began to replace them after the 1914–18 war—contain an undifferentiated proletariat. The single meaningful feature that marks them is their chains (Marx's, this time, not Rousseau's); they are exploited by the bourgeois owners of the means of production. But seen from inside, this population reveals an extraordinary diversity, a multiformity of occupational identities. The neighborhood where I grew up was like that. Top of the heap were those with a "trade"; they had been apprenticed to a master, usually for seven years, before becoming a journeyman carpenter, printer, cabinetmaker, pattern-maker, plumber, electrician, bricklayer, baker, confectioner, tailor, dressmaker, shoemaker, or whatever else. At another level were semiskilled or unskilled workers. There were shop assistants working for the chemist and the chandler and the fishmonger and the greengrocer and the butcher, and laundry workers and riveters and pipefitters and dozens of other positions in shops and factories and offices; and barmaids and draymen and rent collectors and insurance agents and window cleaners and lamplighters and postmen and tram drivers and deliverymen and dockers and bookmaker's runners.

Each occupation, including those considered unskilled, represents an expertise, clearly some more than others, but all of them marking an identity, a person who finds at least part of himself or herself in the skill that the occupation demands. Most of those I knew worked for enterprises, large or small: they were wage earners, not self-employed, persons whose work was monitored by the boss or by the foreman. Most of them also—insurance agent and rent collector and window cleaner are exceptions in the list above—worked more or less under the eye of a supervisor. But for many of them their expertise constituted a barrier that shielded them from supervising authorities. My recollection of expressions of resentment, particularly but not only from journeymen, more often concerned autonomy and expertise than the size of the wage packet or the hours of work. The boss had never done the job, and the foreman had forgotten how to do it, or was never very good at it anyway, and certainly had no right to interfere and certainly did not understand the inescapable constraints that the craft imposed. In short, skill provided an opportunity for disengagement. Workers did it *their* way, not the approved way, either because their way was more efficient, or because it was easier, or both.

Every tradesman had a set of tricks that undercut or short-cut the official procedures for getting things done. Strictly interpreted, this is shirking, breaking regulations that authorities consider to be in the interests of the collective enterprise. The result might be a lemon off the end of the production line or a concrete floor that disintegrates before its time because the workers laid the cement-sand-gravel aggregate dry, when the materials are lighter and easier to shift, and watered it in position. Then the automaker or the construction company may find themselves in court. But that is not always the case. Official procedures cannot take into account all the variables that are encountered on the job; they are sometimes out of date; and often they are drawn up by people who have only had the job described to them but have never done it. In those cases the workers know best, and when they go around the regulations, the consequences may often benefit the enterprise. That this is the case is shown by the form of industrial protest called *working to rule*; by meticulously following every rule in the book, workers can bring the enterprise to a halt.

Disengagement through the exercise of expertise defies the authorities; it is a message to them to keep their noses out. It also gives the worker a sense of identity, of not having alienated his entire self to the bosses. It also suggests that success in making the workforce impeccably obedient may carry with it downstream costs for the enterprise. It is also a reminder that there are limits to the use of compliance. Managers do not have the technical ability, especially when it comes to monitoring and gathering information, to control all aspects of the enterprise.

This sense of autonomy that industrial organization willy-nilly creates is in the same category as the individualism of the scholar or the traveling salesman or Uncle George or the small independent businessman or anyone whose style of life allows them to be their own experts, to make their own decisions. There was a striking example of individualism created by expertise within the four-car troop of armored cars. The most dangerous position was to be in the leading scout car, which had a driver and a commander. If there was an ambush on the road, that car met it first. (This was Europe. The situation in an open terrain like the North African desert was different.) The commander of the leading car, usually a corporal, required some special abilities; map reading of the kind that senses the terrain (rather than just finding the way) and can anticipate where danger might lie; not just good eyesight, but an eye for patterns that will detect something unusual; and an ability to react very quickly, to make an instant decision, on which the life of himself and his driver depended. Some were killed or wounded; some suffered, understandably, from a failure of nerve; some went all the way from Normandy to Hamburg, nerve intact. These men were free, so to speak, made loners and audacious by the peril they faced, very much their own men; anything but mindless; anything but automata; individuals.

But it is not specialization alone, the division of labor, that produces a culture marked by reflexive individualism. The Hindu caste system has a wonderfully baroque division of labor, but, if we follow Dumont, Hinduism downgrades individualism, its nearest equivalent exemplified by the person who has left society and became a Sanyasin (Dumont 1960).[5] Rather what counts is the extent to which specialized skills multiply, the sheer number of them, and the frequency of occasions on which the possessor of a skill becomes his own master by virtue of the skill. The task, the *thing* upon which he operates, insulates him from domination by other people. To that extent, of course, he is dominated, technically rather than morally, by things rather than by other people. Controlled by nature, paradoxically he becomes his own master.

[5]I think he overstates the case. See Mines 1988 and 1990.

But, it may be said, that is a very unusual way to look at industrial society. If the industrial worker has an identity as an individual, that surely is a function not of technical skills but of the much-lamented alienation that is the mark of an industrial workforce. An organization that has no dignity and commands no respect—let alone affection—from its employees and relies mainly on compliance creates conditions that favor disengagement. Rewards or punishments are needed to make alienated workers do what the organization requires, thus creating in them a wholly instrumental attitude towards itself. Treating a person or a collectivity as an instrument is *ipso facto* to refuse to identify oneself with it, and to make oneself separate and independent, and thus to be an individual.

Moreover, to continue the argument, if you must find true individualism somewhere in industrial society, it will surely be among the elite of financial entrepreneurs and venturesome capitalists, the genuinely rugged and amoral individualists, Carnegies and Rockefellers on down to the law-breaking financiers of the late twentieth century. And is it not the case that factory workers become alienated exactly because they are deprived of the chance to show drive and opportunism, even to use their intelligence? Why else would they make "homers?" It may be that a few of them, possessed of relatively rare technical skills, can convince themselves that they are masters of their own working lives. But even then, it could be argued, if the organization is the only place where their skills can be deployed, that is going to commit them to it, make them devoted to it.

I seem to have landed in an imbroglio of conflicting ideas. If, as I claimed, (i) the high level of specialization in industrial society promotes a sense of individuality, can it also be the case that (ii) industrial workers are brainwashed out of any sense of individual identity? Moreover, is it not exactly (iii) alienation, which is the sense of having bartered away oneself to a collectivity, that paradoxically produces the reflexive sense of one's own (lost) distinctiveness? How can one reconcile these various statements?

The middle proposition—that alienated production-line workers turn into zombies—I think is mistaken, and is denied by the third statement. If I see myself used as an instrument, I know that I exist: *abusus aliis, ergo sum.* The first and third statements (which do not contradict one another) are correct and become more persuasive if one compares industrial society with a generic model of its predecessor, peasant society. Remember we are looking for conditions which encourage a person *not* to feel that the whole of life is encompassed within a collectivity.

At first sight the peasant farmer lives a life that should encourage reflexive individualism, together with a sense of self-worth. He does not work on a production line; he is good for any kind of task around the farm, and has many skills. He is not specialized. Moreover he is a decision-maker, and lives with the consequences of what he decides, not of what others tell him to do. The head of a peasant household decides when to sow and when to reap, when to kill the pig, and makes a thousand other management decisions that have to do with the family as well as the farm (marriages, coping with death and with births, and so on); and he joins with others in making decisions that lie with the community, the management of communal property and the organization of the community's festivals.

But these decisions are of a peculiar kind. They are closely regulated by natural events and by custom. In fact the decisions are not markers of individualism, because they are routinized and standardized; they are the kind of decisions the peasant's father made, and his son will make, and his neighbors also make. They are part of an unchanging rhythm of life that is found in any place that combines agricultural production with a constant technology. They are part of a life-style that is validated by tradition and by ritual, invested with dignity. From this perspective the peasant on his farm and even in his community comes near to being as regimented and mindless as the well-trained soldier on the parade ground; perhaps more so since the peasant's training begins in the cradle.

Why is this not equally true of workers on a production line, who do not even appear to make their own decisions? (Decisions are made for them by the machine and its designers.) There are very clear differences between peasants and industrial workers. What workers do is not hallowed by tradition. Theirs is not an unthinking *acceptance* of a way of life as legitimate, or perhaps as inevitable, as God's design, but a reluctant *compliance* with the orders of human superiors, a compliance that is partly forced and partly purchased. Furthermore, they are unlikely to be doing what their parents did or their children will do; they do not learn a skill from one generation and pass it on to the next.[6] All around them other people are doing other things; that is the nature of a production line. The essential and detailed similarities that make for a sense of an encompassing collectivity are present in the peasant's life but are absent from the proletarian life. The peasants can talk to each other about the work they do and how they are faring. What shop talk gets exchanged between a meat packer and a Linotype operator? What do they have in common apart, perhaps, from industrial grievances or ways of beating the system?

Production lines notwithstanding, industrial society has created an immense diversity of skills, albeit often minor skills acquired without much effort, that did not exist in peasant life. It has much diminished the sense that I am like others in the

---

[6]There are, of course, industrial situations in which that pattern occurs, although less frequently now than in the past. Company towns, mining areas, and shipbuilding all had firms in which two or even three generations worked at the same job. In those places, predictably, disengagement arising from the spirit of isolated individualism that I am discussing, was less evident than collective, activist, discontent.

way I live and work, both within a generation and across generations and across neighborhoods and to an extent even in the same factory. Second, it has produced the sense that, since I am not like others, I should not be compared with them as better or worse. My difference is the source of my self-respect. True, others may be richer than I am and may tell me what to do, but that is not part of the moral order: it is a technical or possibly a political matter. Their dominance in the workplace, if technically based, should not give them the right to a generalized moral superiority.

Third, paradoxically, although I am on a production line or turned into the appendage of a machine and more or less mindlessly occupied, I am neither a mindless servant of the organization that employs me, like a soldier in the army is supposed to be, nor am I mindlessly encompassed in an all-consuming way of life, like a peasant. My moral being, while certainly not unaffected by the organization, is intact enough to let me attend to other obligations, perhaps by becoming an activist in the proletarian cause, or by allowing those many loyalties that I care about—family, religion, sport, whatever—to create me, an individual, a point of intersection between diverse and sometimes conflicting moral obligations. To the extent that the organization blocks these aspirations, it invites dissidence. To the extent that it can also penalize dissidence, it invites svejkism.

Fourth, and not least, as a worker in an industrial setting I am driven, like the sixth-former, to see my individuality in my encounter with things, not with people. The "people" that frustrate me are not really people, but abstract things. Haraszti's furious eloquence is directed much less against the bosses in the tractor factory than against the system, the "norm." Certainly, outside the context of the shop floor, I know that the time-and-motion expert is a person, a moral being, something more than just his expertise. The experience of piecework tells me not to see him that way, but to depersonalize him, to see him as the appendage of a machine, to deny him moral standing. I make an object out of him, just as he makes an object out of me. I am not part of him, nor is he part of me, nor are we together morally encompassed by a collectivity. We are individuals in conflict. Certainly we each ally ourselves with others so as to fight more effectively and in those alliances there may be a strong morality. But *our* interaction has no morality to guide it; it is wholly instrumental, because we are the intersecting point of two separate and opposed moralities.[7]

That is how we come to see ourselves as individuals and how we remain, to some degree, outside the collectivity. Our ideas are the product of our experience, and that experience varies. It varies ultimately with the varied acts of God. Proximately, it varies with the collectivities that, through their conventions and the people who control them, seek to dominate our lives. Whether a collectivity promotes its own dignity or whether it is forced to make concessions to the dignity of individuals varies with what it does in the world, what its task is, and how legitimate the task is. To that question I now turn, beginning with the effects of varying institutional legitimacy.

TRADING DIGNITY FOR EFFICIENCY

Training for the Oxbridge scholarship race was also a training in reflexive self-awareness. But sixth-formers, destined (we hoped) to gain university entrance, were only about 10 percent of the school's enrollment. A proportion of those in lower forms (labeled *Alpha* on the classical side and *A* on the

---

[7]To see the significant enemy in the system rather than the person reverses the process, described in chapter three, in which symbolic disrespect is directed at the sergeant-major rather than the regiment. This difference, to the extent that it exists, indicates that the army did a better job of manufacturing its own dignity than most economic enterprises manage to do.

modern studies or science side) were pointed in the direction of the sixth forms and university education. But there were also marginal people in *B* or *Beta* forms, and others probably over the margin in C or *Gamma* forms, and still others certainly beyond redemption in forms labeled *D* or *Remove* or *Transitus*. They were destined to leave at sixteen and go into clerking jobs in commerce or banking or local government, qualifying themselves by passing the lower school certificate, a regionally administered public examination. The same examination, taken at a higher level, was called matriculation and to pass it was an entry into the sixth form. Those who failed were destined for less-than-university careers (no one was tactful enough in those days to say "*other*-than-university"). Given that they constituted about four-fifths of pupils below sixth-form level, it is clear that either there had to be more than one definition of the school's task, or, if the definition remained purportedly all-encompassing, the task would not command the same legitimacy in all quarters. It did not. The happy coincidence of ambition that existed between the school and the sixth-formers was certainly not found among those who "failed," that is, those who did not show the required academic excellence. Many of them could not wait to get out of the place and find a job, and regretted that they had not been allowed to leave school at fourteen, like boys who attended elementary schools, and who were already wearing cloth caps, earning money, and losing their virginity.

I have no hard evidence that boys in the leave-at-sixteen category were more disengaged than were the sixth-formers. But I suspect many of them were. They were certainly more given to noncompliance; there were more disciplinary problems, more punishments handed out among them than among sixth-formers. They were rowdy on the tramcars, they stuffed their school caps into their pockets when they got fifty yards away from the school building (What pre-adult is not embarrassed by a schoolboy's cap?), and occasionally little gangs were caught shoplifting in the lunch break (for which they were expelled). Except for those few who were good at games, gaining places on the school teams, and were therefore incorporated into the "institutional dignity" side of the school's activities, the early-leavers were disenchanted, because the school's dominant value (academic success, measured by university entrance) had no meaning for them.

The disaffected "failures," while certainly not encompassed by the school and its values, were for the most part not exemplifiers of individualism. In the resistance they put up to the school and its academic values few of them were loners. Mischief or defiance was usually a joint affair, and even when there was a single perpetrator of some genial outrage (for example, profanity scrawled on the blackboard or a stink bomb let off in assembly) there were always others to support him ("egg him on to it"). The code against revealing the identity of a wrongdoer ("snitching") was very strict. In other words, and quite in accordance with my argument, the disaffected schoolboys mostly lived in a world of the "gang" or the "peer group," the sixth-formers much less so.

With respect to the legitimacy of the dominant value, my army experience was very different. The dominant value really did transcend. Like most of my fellow soldiers, I knew why I was there—to fight a war—and rejection of that obligation never crossed our minds. For most ordinary people in Britain the Second World War was, at worst, an unfortunate necessity; for some it was a crusade, and to fight in it was a privilege. In the same way activists who now fight to save the environment, or who work in a peace movement, or who protest a woman's right to have an abortion, or who protest the protesters, do not require performative manipulation to make them show devotion to the organization. The devotion is already there and the theater they put on has less to do with manufacturing devotion than with intimidating an opposition. Organizations that acquire legitimacy from the legitimacy of the task are "movements," a word that signifies mindless and unshiftable faith in the rightness of the cause. It is this faith that allows some of them to survive inept management and the transparent failure to achieve their stated goals, despite the fact that the members, unlike soldiers, are volunteers and free any time to detach themselves. These are the conditions which greatly favor holism and tend to cut back on awareness of individual distinctiveness.

In contrast with the 1939–45 war, the Anglo-French invasion of Egypt eleven years later was, for about half of Britain's population, an immoral act and an egregious stupidity. The conscript army that was in being for a few years after the 1939–45 war in Britain, a country that does not have a tradition of compulsory military service, was a disenchanted army because the conscripts saw themselves paying an unwarranted opportunity cost: they could have been getting on with their lives. The adolescents who were forced to stay in school until the statutory leaving age, failing to acquire academic skills that they did not want anyway, had just the same feeling. Disenchantment also sets in when skills are left unused. The *Guardian* (August 1, 1990) reported that British soldiers who did not have the good fortune to risk their lives in Ulster felt inadequate.[8]

All these varieties of disenchantment are likely to be noticed by those who control the institutions, and they can react in a variety of ways that have different effects on reflexive individualism. First, dignity may sometimes be quietly shelved and compliance used in place of consent. A pointless task need not

---

[8]The same report gave a vivid description of drunkenness, violence, and some unspeakably barbaric initiation rites. The soldiers whom I knew in wartime certainly boozed when they had the chance; but I remember neither hazing nor much mindless hooliganism, and the portrait of contemporary military life was one that I did not recognize. Then there was neither time nor need for such perverted dignity-making rituals as bootblacking a recruit's testicles or inflicting other even less amiable sexual humiliations.

then lead to disaffection. For example, a bureaucracy that concocts pointless work to justify its existence will not suffer from disaffection among the workers, if it pays them enough. Such workers are not disaffected, but they are likely to be disengaged and see themselves, reflexively, as individuals with individual interests. They do not internalize the organization's official image of itself and when it suits them they covertly break both the spirit and the letter of its regulations.

Second, a bureaucracy may resort to the mindless sacralizing of its own dignity, in order to combat disenchantment. The bank employees I knew in India would have thought that their world was coming apart, if a customer could go to the bank (I speak of the 1950s) and draw cash on a letter of credit without signing his name thirteen times, drinking six cups of tea, and spending not less than two hours. Attention to detail is what matters, they would have said, and corners must not be cut. Bureaucratic theater then becomes a way of life and bureaucratic interactions are transformed, in a quite literal way, into a form of play that, like any game, liberates the players from mundane obligations, which in this case is doing the job that the organization was created to do. Insofar as the theater is convincing, reflexive individualism is inhibited.

When dignity stands in for efficiency, those who control the organization may be aware of what is happening, but they are unlikely to admit it. They say that the true purpose of the organization has now been made clear and its task has been constructively redefined. What previously were to be suppressed as pagan festivals turn out to be primitive versions of Christian rites; the festivals, renamed, can perfectly well be incorporated into the Church's calendar. A government regulatory agency, set up to curb the excesses of an industry and unable or unwilling to do so, quietly redefines its role as a facilitator and promoter of good relations between government and the industry. A peacetime army, largely concerned with pomp and ceremony, will still insist that it is the nation's defender and execute summer maneuvers to show its readiness for (the last) war. Again, if the bluff succeeds, reflexive individualism is discouraged. If it fails, the scene is nicely set for flanneling.

A similar pretense is required when dignity is tacitly put on one side in the interests of efficiency, but this time the pretense promotes reflexive individualism. If the master of the lower sixth, knowing that we cheated, had put a stop to it, he would have been elevating dignity over efficiency. If the army had insisted that the "dignity" stirrup pump (the one kept polished, as distinct from the one that had been scrounged) should be used for fire drills, that, paradoxical as it sounds, would also have been to put dignity before efficiency. If the school authorities had applied the same academic standards to the Remove forms or the C and D streams as they did to the top stream and had tried to enforce their demands (the same amount of homework, the same smaller classes, and so forth), that too would have been to substitute dignity for efficiency (the publicized value, in this instance, would have been a populist egalitarianism in place of the rampant Oxbridge-oriented elitism). In all those cases rules would have been sanctified at the price of accomplishment, a sacrifice that is self-destructive when the task (winning the war, getting scholarships to Oxbridge) is what mostly gives the organization its legitimacy. In these circumstances institutional dignity can be maintained only if room is given also for personal dignity, for individualism.

Tasks that make the institution's boundaries porous also put devotion at risk and sharpen the sense of individual distinctiveness. A monastic order that has a rule of seclusion should find it easier to preserve the habit of innocent faith than do other orders, such as the Benedictines, which work in the world. Roman Catholic parish priests or members of Opus Dei and similar organizations, being outside the cloister, are more open to temptation and worldly corruption. This does not mean that parish priests habitually run away with the Children of Mary, or that all Opus Dei executives become corrupt right-wing politicians; it means only that the context in which they work makes it more difficult to sustain devotion to the letter of Catholic ideology. Sometimes this situation leads to a form of svejkism—a re-emergence of individual initiative—that resembles our cheating over tests in the lower sixth. The organization's *main* values are preserved, the corner-cutters claim, even if the organization has a rule against cutting those corners. There have, for example, been egregious scandals in the Vatican, perpetrated by people who appear to have remained devoted in their service to the Catholic church (Gurvin 1984 or Yallop 1985).

Contact with outsiders, the risk of contaminating dignity, and the likelihood of a stronger sense of individual self-awareness vary with the organization's task. Location is one factor. The office worker who sits day-in and day-out at a desk, doing routine things, is not only more vulnerable to measures enforcing compliance than, say, the traveling salesman or the skilled technician, but also is more available for theatrical routines that induce consent. But theater is also important in the opposite situation, when members have skills or occupations that preclude close supervision (as with scholars, research workers, or traveling salesmen), and monitoring costs are high enough to make theater a better investment. The sales force is called in to conferences and seminars. Senior civil servants in Britain, generously paid with a salary that is inflexibly linked to rank and thus rules out money as an extra incentive, are rewarded with the dignity of a "K," the knighthood that transforms mere "Appleby" to "Sir Humphrey." In commerce, industry, the arts, and journalism, awards for outstanding work are not unceremoniously mailed out to the winners; they become centerpieces for ceremonies that sometimes are lavish to the point of vulgarity (especially those of the performing arts, where, since everyone is a diva, a sense of the collectivity does not come easily). As with the school assembly or the annual prize-giving, the collectivity, its values, its members, and their relative ranking, are then made visible not only to members themselves but also to the outside world. Priests are summoned out of their parishes to a retreat, where they renew and strengthen their vows of loyalty to the Church and its doctrines. The university's diverse array of administrators are taken out to a resort to spend a weekend together holding a "workshop" that ostensibly addresses technical administrative problems, but in reality also serves to create a sense of community and mutual dependence. Even the people who run the parking services are supposed to come back feeling they are not entirely out of "the body."

Incarceration, literal or ideological, also has an intellectual dimension. Schools or universities, which are intended to foster individual talent, are denied the freedom that armies or monastic orders have to make their members mindless automata. A cloistered order like the Carmelite nuns, whose task is prayer, requires a mind-set that is different from an order that takes on the world at its own secular games, like the Jesuits. The task then may be such that it cannot be performed by someone who has been rendered mindless by his devotion to the institution. There is, it is again clear, an inherent tension between devotion and tasks that require intelligence.

To be made to think for yourself is to be an individual; not to think for yourself is to be encompassed within a collectivity. Organizations that have a task in the world to that extent have difficulty in preventing their members from being contaminated by loyalties directed elsewhere. They may also be required, on pain of being unable to carry out their task in the world, to enhance their members' capacity to think for themselves. Exactly where holism is traded for individualism, in those circumstances, will depend upon how far the organization can turn itself into an institution: that is, into a collectivity that is intrinsically valued for itself, rather than for the task that it performs in the world. The outcome depends not only on the strategies followed by leaders of the collectivities, but also on the collectivity's own intrinsic nature and on the wider context that constrains it.

Chapter 6

Split Vision

Where the individual, no longer squandered
  In self-assertion, works with the rest, endowed
With the split vision of a juggler and the quick lock of a
taxi. . . .

—Louis MacNeice, "Autumn Journal"

SPLIT VISION

Armies and schools and colleges must work hard to earn dignity and become institutions instead of mere organizations, thus being recognized as ends in themselves and commanding selfless service. Businesses must work even harder. But there is one institution that, taking different forms in different cultures, yet everywhere appears to command intrinsic regard: it is the family, an exemplification, *par excellence*, of Rousseau's chains.

Any collectivity that is intrinsically valued inhibits reflexive individualism. It does so by definition; *intrinsic* means that members are not supposed to look to their own interests or their own dignity, but to subordinate both in the service of the institution. In the real world no institution, not even the family, manages to eliminate individualism to that extent. There is everywhere a split vision. The two values, reflexive individualism and holism, are always present and always in complementary distribution; as one rises the other falls.

I have assumed that the relative distribution of holistic and individualistic attitudes in any population is a dependent variable, changing as events and people's experience change.[1] Events and experience in the end decide which, among competing collectivities, will be the object of devotion, and also decide how strongly devotion will diminish or be diminished by reflexive individualism. They do not do so instantly; people hold on religiously to ideas and values that experience teaches them are no longer tenable. More specifically, devotion to a particular collectivity (or the lack of it) is ultimately a function of how people are organized to make a living and of how power is distributed. Those features in turn are affected by the larger events of history. Within those parameters, I have looked at various ways in which the distribution of the two kinds of attitude can be manipulated; what the leaders of organizations or institutions do to increase devotion; and what penalties they pay if they are too successful in suppressing individual initiatives.

In this final chapter I look at the larger constraints that set limits to this manipulation. I first examine a strongly internalized holistic value—that placed on the family in our culture—in order to reconsider my central assumption, asking whether such values are, in some degree, responsive to the world of experience. I think they are, but not readily so. Lessons are slowly learned. In the second part of the chapter I revisit some of the settings that occurred earlier in the book, with the intention of showing how the experience of events moved people, most of whom had responded positively to wartime demands for holism, back toward a consciousness of

---

[1] I take as given that for certain collectivities, notably the family, psychophysical variables underlie and set limits to the determinants provided by experience. See Spiro 1980.

themselves as individuals, standing apart from, and sometimes defiantly against, collectivities. Here too people did not manage an immediate adjustment to a changed world.

THE CONTEXT OF DOMINATION

A family is small, face-to-face, and supposedly founded on a rock of moral solidarity. It is an end in itself. A family is not looked upon as an instrument designed by someone to get something done, and therefore expendable if some better device can be produced to do the job.[2] Also, in the context of a family there are no impersonal interactions. All exchanges are personal; all should be founded on trust; all should be legitimate, because altruism is the rule. The sensible worker on the shop floor anticipates exploitation, because that is the nature of his relationship with the bosses. Peasants expect to be oppressed by the gentry, because that is the nature of their society. But parents exploiting children and husbands exploiting wives act *unnaturally* (that is, immorally). In the real world, of course, those things happen. Some cases, being outrageous, are easily recognized. Others are harder to detect because everyone assumes that authority in the family must be benevolent, not exploitative, because that is how things naturally are. The family, so to speak, is pre-adjusted for devotion; and devotion should cancel out the resentment that domination otherwise would bring. *A fortiori*, disengagement, whether symbolic or practical, should be quite uncommon.

It is therefore a paradox that family life is proverbially in-

---

[2]This attitude persists despite the fact that the family in our culture has progressively yielded more and more of its earlier functions to the state and other institutions. There have been experiments, the best known of which is the Israeli kibbutz. See Spiro 1963 and 1980. The second book charts the limits within which family form responds to contextual changes.

flected with the harshest of negative emotions. "Your brother is your real enemy," the Oriyas say. In Ivy Compton-Burnett's novels one gets the feeling that under the floorboards even the mice are bickering with one another like the family members above.[3] I recall a semidocumentary film about Everton football (soccer) fans. The young husband had chosen to go with his mates to an away match at the time his wife was to have their first child. We see him return to the house, still wearing his supporters' scarf and a funny hat with the blue and white Everton rosette pinned to it, and, slightly drunk and a little shamefaced, put his head round the bedroom door to a room full of women: his mother, his sister, his wife's mother, his wife, and his new daughter. "Hello, love. Alright then?" answered with "You bloody rotten swine!" from his wife, and "She don't want you in here" from one of the older women.

That sentence "She don't want you in here" can stand as an allegory for the paradox of family life. She may not want him, but, their culture says, they are bound together by ties that are far more compelling than mere enlightened self-interest, like the worker and the boss. They are a family, man and wife and children all willingly shackled by the chains, the conventions, of family life. That is one part of the culture to which peasants and Everton's working-class fans subscribe; the family is a transcending unit and all its members are equal in their subordination to it. The other part of the culture states quite plainly that all are *not* equal: men rank above women and the old should have deference from the young.

There is an extensive mythology that purports to explain why, at least on the front stage of these cultures, men are effortlessly superior to women. There are also various quasi-rational economistic theories that link biological difference and reproductive roles to the allocation of economic and political

[3]This pleasantry comes from a conversation, many years ago, with the late Franz Steiner.

tasks. Most of them are persuasive only at the level of very elementary modeling; women's productive capacities are lessened by pregnancy and the care of small children. Disqualifications above that level speak less to economically rational arrangements than to vested interests and power. Psychobiological differences, entirely divorced from cultural factors, will not explain why there has yet to be a woman president of the United States.[4] But that kind of grand theorizing, which is the core of the evolutionary model of status-free exchange and the rational society, is not my present concern. My question speaks to context rather than cause: not "Why are men dominant?" but "What else went along with this ideology of male dominance?"

In the working-class culture that I knew half a century ago there were certain stereotypes that bespoke both enmity between men and women and their mutual contempt. It was a world marked by sexism, in both directions. A man, even if he was a "good provider" and a "good father" and did not booze and did not use violence on his wife or children, nevertheless belonged to the category *male*, which inescapably connoted collective silliness (like football fans), failure to contribute properly to the household, the abuse of domestic power, and a readiness to make instrumental use of women and their services, whether sexual or domestic. A good husband was only an exception and did not invalidate the generalized image of the male as vile, dominating, and exploitative. Working-class behavior even years later matched this description of standard maleness. Read Willis's account (1981) of "the lads," working-class youths in Britain, and the distinction they made between the "missus" (the steady girlfriend) and other girls, who exist only to be seduced; manhood is to be found, among other ac-

---

[4]The *Los Angeles Times* (Feb. 5, 1991) reports that a male passenger, discovering as the plane left the gate that the pilot was a woman, insisted on being let off.

tivities (such as thieving, fighting, and defying authority), in violating women.[5]

The matching stereotype of women had just the same division between the good woman (exemplified by mother or sister or sometimes wife) and women in general, who were a source of evil. The good woman in this culture was hardworking, nurturant, and loyal in adversity (loyal to her family), and her identity was founded in her family and household. But those were the exceptions, particular women. Women in general were manipulative, sexually aberrant (oversexed or undersexed), titillating and provocative when young, fat and domineering in middle age, cantankerous in old age, ludicrous in their demands, stupid around machinery, crassly ignorant about sport, and not to be trusted in the public domain. Worst of all, while naturally inferior they nevertheless resented male superiority and would undermine it when they could. This attitude toward women is well caught and caricatured in vulgar postcards, still sold in seaside resorts in Britain.

What was it in everyday life that made such stereotypes possible for men and women who were bound to one another by the closest of moral ties? My argument will be that the patterns of activity within the family and household were such that they loosened the emotional bonds of family life, and thus approximated the other person to a stereotype that permitted instrumentality. By *emotional* bonds I do not mean the dramatic and intense emotion of sexual love; rather I refer to companionship and a trust that is absolutely not calculating. Household activity, in working-class culture at that time in those places, was so structured that it made for the perception of difference,

[5]Willis presents this image, Studs Terkel fashion, in the boys' own words, as if it were the reality. I can recall a few boys who did in fact live out the *macho* near-criminal image, but they were not the majority and they were not admired. But people talked, disapprovingly, as if the stereotype were the common reality.

mutual wariness, and therefore also for individual detachment from the chains of family conventions. It is a situation somewhat reminiscent of the worker and the boss. Even if you are lucky and have a boss who is kind and considerate, he must be an exception, and you can surely expect him from time to time to revert to type and be exploitative. I will argue that the pattern of family activities tended to keep similar perceptions alive, despite the emotional bonding supposedly inherent in family life.

Working-class life in Britain between the wars was marked by a quite ritualistic division of labor, a pretense about what work was "naturally" in the domain of one or the other sex. I recall the mixture of consternation and amusement in my father's older sister when she saw her nephew change a baby's diaper. Men did not cook; men did not clean house; men did not wash clothes or sew on buttons or darn socks or knit; some men were tidy but a man who failed to "pick up after himself" around the house was just being a man. Men did not go shopping for household supplies, unless the wife was incapacitated. A man could walk in the park with his wife and the baby in a pram, but the wife pushed the pram. There was a similar list of tabooed work for women; a woman who could do minor carpentry or plumbing or nail up a fence was a nine-days-wonder and a bit comical. It seems almost as if the culture mistrusted the efficacy of moral cohesion and chose to reinforce family solidarity by an exaggerated division of labor, thus making man and wife *materially*, rather than emotionally, dependent on each other (and in the process undermining moral cohesion). Tasks that were parceled between men and women for conventional rather than technical reasons increased mutual dependency. It was firmly believed that no widower could run a household without a woman, a sister or a mother or a daughter or a hired housekeeper, and that widows were hard put to it if they did not have a brother or a grown son or some other man around to help with men's work. This division of labor, while enhancing Durkheim's *organic* solidarity, diminished his other kind of solidarity, *mechanical*, which rests on a perception of like situation, of being in the same boat.

The culturally constituted pattern of leisure activities pushed in the opposite direction, making men and women *not* dependent on one another. But the effect was the same: to make an inroad on the moral (that is, emotional) dependency of man and wife. Women got their support from other women: mothers, sisters, daughters, and, much less securely, from women connected to them through their men, brothers' wives and their networks. But even the mother-in-law could be counted on for support in some male-versus-female altercations, as in the case of the Everton football fan. Men's solidarity was with other men, their "mates," those friends whom they could trust and in whom they confided. Men's hobbies, with the exception of gardening or doing handyman work around the house, took them outside the family, and the wife who shared the hobby was the exception rather than the rule. It was, in short, the world that is caricatured by Andy Capp—beer, sports, betting, and pigeon racing for the man, and tea-drinking and gossip and toil for the woman, all of it permeated by an ambivalent mutual hostility. Even joint visits to the pub see them separated: him standing at the bar and her sitting with other women. Men's ties with other men, and women's with other women, substituted for the moral and emotional needs that might otherwise have been met within the household.

In both these ways the sentiment of family devotion that might have whitewashed the facts of exploitation and domination is diminished. The household can more easily be seen as an enterprise, a kind of business, the males and the older members being the bosses in charge of the females and the junior members. The exercise of power becomes visible more as power and less as authority (legitimate power), and the stage is set for disengagement. It should be remembered, however, that, in the context of a family, domination and disengagement are not easily insulated from the discourse of duty and of conscience.

The marked division of labor in the household gave women control over their own legitimate space and endowed them with the autonomy of expertise—"Stay out of my kitchen!" It also facilitated both evasion and enclaving (doing things one's own way and at one's own pace, whatever the boss says). The households that I recall ran on cash, not checkbooks. At that time few married women with children had regular outside jobs. The man was the "breadwinner." Exceptionally—enough to be remarked upon—the man handed over his unopened wage packet and received pocket money from his wife. More commonly she got housekeeping money, but how she disposed of it was her business, and it was expected that a smart wife would build up her own reserve fund, her "nest egg." If the nest egg turned out to be larger than a man had anticipated, that could cause trouble. If she used it in ways that benefited outsiders rather than herself or her own household, that too might cause a row.

Second, the purportedly noninstrumental nature of family life made it legitimate for a woman to resist the demands not only of the man, but even of the household itself, for reasons of infirmity. The physiology of reproduction was peculiarly effective in this way. Male culture allowed, with some reluctance, that for a period each month a woman might not perform as a woman should and that there was not much to be done about it. There was a particular mystery built around a woman's reproductive organs and their working, entirely separated from their sexual aspects. There were no dirty jokes about the birth canal or about breastfeeding. There were some about menstruation, but generally considered "mucky" or "a bit much." Copulation apart, the events of reproduction belonged in the private domain of women, and no man, other than a doctor, was ever present at childbirth, unless by accident. The Everton football fan got into trouble not because he was not in the bedroom for the delivery, but because he was not somewhere close at hand, displaying anxiety and concern.

Third, symbolic disengagement from a man's authority often took the form of a statement about duty. The language of holism was used to justify a woman's individual rights. Authority figures were not evaded or defied, but made to feel guilty. A similar device (outside the family) is found in peasant and industrial societies, where it usually takes the form of appealing to compassion, to *noblesse oblige*, the obligation of the powerful to help those less fortunate than themselves. The tone between men and women in the family is different; it is not an appeal to generosity, it is less deferential than it is accusatory, more a complaint that the other person is not sufficiently moved by his (occasionally her) obligations to the family and the household. They are not being asked to go the extra mile; they are being accused of slacking. Material failures are translated into moral inadequacy. Money spent on betting and drinking, at the expense of the family's needs; money spent on "fancy" women; time that belongs to the family spent elsewhere as in "You use this house like it was a hotel!" (that one more for teenage children than for husbands); even blameless failure to provide, through unemployment, could all be indicators of a failed identity and an occasion for nagging, complaining, and the entailed reminder that those who fail to perform as family heads forfeit authority and justify, indeed make inevitable, disengagement.

Mostly these complaints did not stay within the household but were transmitted through neighbors and especially relatives, going from one woman to another gossiping over the back fence, or walking to the shops, or sharing a pot of tea in the kitchen.[6] In this way the network of emotional support between women was mobilized, and the defaulters, like the Everton supporter, were subjected to a display of collective contempt. At that point of open confrontation, the boundary between disengagement and opposition has been crossed. But it is opposition to a *particular* man because he is flawed and has failed to conduct himself in a way that would justify his exercise of authority. It leaves intact the convention that in the ideal family authority belongs with the male *as the provider*. "He is a good provider," people said, using the appellation that could also be used for God. In that respect nagging is not resistance to conventions but rather a complaint about the misuse of power; it protests the individual, not the system.

The system is the family as a moral enclave, an institution that, like the formal organizations described earlier, seeks to center all loyalties on itself. Unlike those associations, it does not need to organize brainwashing as part of a conscious hegemonic strategy; moral supremacy is, so to speak, innate, a part of the culture that normal people take for granted. When formal organizations compete with one another for the services of their members, church and state, perhaps, or corporations in competition in the market, that is just competition, an interesting process to be dispassionately analyzed. But when one of them competes with a family, or when families compete with one another (as women in many societies are torn between their natal families and the family into which they have married, or in the tensions that arise from in-law intrusions), the atmosphere changes. Dispassionate analysis, of course, is still possible, but it is difficult because a hugely emotional element

[6]Domestic refrigerators were unknown and shopping was done at least once a day. "Running" was the verb used, suggesting pressing domestic obligations and drawing a veil over the gossiping that went on, while walking to the shops or standing in the street.

is injected into the situation, making the subject better suited for the subtle nuancing of fiction than for sociology.

We have strong feelings, both positive and negative, about families, feelings that belong in the domain of the unspoken, the taken-for-granted, the "natural." All our institutions come under attack from time to time—the monarchy, politicians, schools and universities, the military, the civil service, business corporations, capitalism, socialism, and so forth. Every attack brings some furious true-believer out of the woodwork to proclaim "This is sinful!" or "This is madness!" or to talk about the end of civilization as we know it, which provokes opposing true-believers into reciprocal extravagances. But open attacks on the family as an institution—the anthropologist Edmund Leach once did it in a series of BBC lectures—go mostly unsupported. It is the case of the emperor and his new clothes, and only the very innocent can speak the truth. Sensible people pretend they have no chains, at least in public. An American television documentary that centered on family disharmony was a source of immense public discomfort. The cow is just that much too sacred and, if the seamier side of family life is to be exposed, it had better be done in a literary than a scientific framework. Scientific statements are general; literature concerns the particular and the reader or viewer can always find comfort in the thought that this must be an exception, and anyway it is fiction. Alternatively the truth can be acted out by deserting the family and finding emotional solace elsewhere.

Nevertheless there is a constant everyday unspoken protest against the system, and it is being made by both women and men. Disengagement, of the kind described, is not only from persons misusing authority but also from the institution itself, from Rousseau's chains. The emotional bonding between women and other women, and between men and other men, and the conventionalized hostility between men and women as categories, are all forms of disengagement from the moral authority of the family as an institution. *Disengagement* is exactly the word because there is no overt and conscious attempt to demolish the institution. The disengagers are doing what shirkers and cheats and others do in formal organizations; they are marking a territory where the writ of the institution should not run, keeping it in its place so to speak, while implicitly acknowledging that it has a place and is not expendable. They, men and women both, are reserving the right to invest some of their emotional resources outside the family.

Resentment of the family as an institution is mostly precluded from public expression. Husbands and wives fight, but this hostility is given *symbolic* expression only outside the family context and in a highly conventionalized way through a discourse about the behavioral shortcomings of the *category* of men and the *category* of women. The expression of hostility between the sexes is conventionalized, and in that way it functions almost as carnival does, a safety valve that allows the unsayable to be openly said. What cannot be said about the nature of the family may safely be said about the nature of males and females. Of course that does not protect particular families from the consequences of putting their members in chains. Some families break up and others live in a bear-pit. It merely leaves intact the Platonic form, the cultural image of the essential goodness of family life.

REFLEXIVE INDIVIDUALISM AND WORK EXPERIENCE

I have conceptually distinguished between disengagement from the institution and disengagement from dominant males. Both men and women surreptitiously resent the chains of the institution; women at the same time resent their subordination to males. Women resent the python-like qualities of the institution and want space of their own (a condition now called "stir-crazy"), but they also and, perhaps less ambivalently, resent their subordinate position in the institution. That kind of resentment is being more and more openly expressed, as the economic context of working-class families changes.

The working-class world where the man was the breadwinner; where women, if they worked at all, worked part time for money that was called "extra" and was never enough to be a living wage; where the labor of the household was rigidly divided; where acknowledged emotional intimacy between husband and wife that was more than sex was thought somewhat exceptional (brother and sister, at a pinch, might be "pals," but not so often husband and wife); where men trusted men (ironically, their "mates"), and women trusted their mothers and sisters and a network of neighborhood women—that world has been in a slow decline since the 1939–45 war, in proportion to the growing numbers of women in the work force and the full-time jobs open to them.

There is no mystery about the conditions in which men hold the dominant position in a family. *Formal* dominance (I am not speaking of strong and weak personalities) invariably goes either with the man being the exclusive breadwinner or, if he is not, with the confinement of women to the household. There is clear evidence from a variety of cultures that male dominance goes with keeping women at home. The woman can still be engaged in productive labor and make a vital contribution to household income, as is the case with peasant wives; but since their work is under the general direction of the husband or father and in an enterprise that is controlled by him, they remain subservient. How true this is becomes obvious when peasant women manage market enterprises outside the home; they are conspicuously independent in their attitudes and occasionally boisterously disrespectful toward men.

Sometimes the confinement is very literal. The Muslim-inspired institution of purdah that still to some extent characterizes Hindu northern India can only work when the household is rich enough to support nonproductive women. These women do not work in the fields, or take jobs outside the home, and their movements out of the house are strictly supervised. Even inside the home there is often little to do beyond supervising the work of servants, and only over those servants and their own daughters and daughters-in-law do women have authority. Some of them may have influence, but it can be exercised only through the grace and favor of a male. Total seclusion and subordination through privileged idleness becomes less feasible as male-controlled household income diminishes and women's contribution to the productive process becomes more and more necessary. At the other end of the scale in India the women of certain untouchable castes, who work as day laborers and are the family's breadwinners no less than their husbands, exhibit a robust independence and a readiness to treat their union with a man as an enterprise in which it makes sense to get rid of a bad provider and find a better one.[7] In other words, some of Rousseau's chains tend to snap when they are seen to be the cause of sufficient material discomfort.

The idealized norm of a traditional working-class household (the male as breadwinner and in control, the wife subordinated and a homemaker) is only possible if the man, like those rich Indians, brings home enough money to support his family. But the great majority of working men are wage earners, employed by enterprises that are moved exclusively by profit, that is, by buying cheap and selling dear. Enterprises have a constant incentive to hire the cheapest efficient labor they can find, and wage levels are not determined by the notion of what it costs to set up worker families in the back street equivalent of purdah. Moreover, if the supply of labor can be increased by employing females, the unit price of labor should go down. Then women are pulled out of the home and removed from the domain in which their husband rules, and in which they are bound by family conventions, and thrust into a different do-

[7]Gough 1956:844–49.

main in which the relationships are not moral (as in the family) but instrumental. That domain, moreover, has no ideology about what constitutes a proper family; the basic principle involved, as has been remarked at least since the time of Adam Smith, who worried about the breakdown of family life, is that of industrial capitalism (and of our evolutionary model)—productive efficiency.

Notice what this does to the woman who takes a job in a factory or in an office. First, her position in the household is no longer one that rests entirely on family moral convention, on the basis, that is, of her being the wife and mother. Now, with a job and a wage packet to bring home, she begins to be like an investor in an enterprise. Furthermore, the attitudes that belong in the office or the shop may be transported into the home and may infect its relationships with a taint of instrumentality. There is an invitation to accounting and comparing contributions (which are very comparable since money is involved) that was not there before.

Second, the division of labor inside the home is also threatened. There is now a rational argument for altering the pattern of domestic work to make allowances for the fact that both husband and wife spend forty hours a week working outside the home. Work in the home must either be redefined to fit the fewer hours the woman has available for it, or it must be shared by the man, or both, or (not usually a working-class solution, or even much a middle-class one at the present day) servants fill the gap. We are anything but instantly rational in matters such as this, but men have certainly become more ambidextrous around the home than they were in my father's day, and it is expected of them.[8] The shift is also helped out by technology, such as new household machinery, by ways of

[8]But not everywhere. In urban Croatia, where women work in factories, the men have mostly not become domesticated. Grandmothers, especially the wife's mother, help out. See Gilliland 1986.

heating that do not make everything filthy, and by the habit of eating out (the functional equivalent of which was always there in the form of the neighborhood chip shop, too frequent recourse to which got a woman a reputation for being a slattern.) The effect of this sharing of the housework (or exporting it) is to create one more resemblance between men and women, and so to provide a basis for the kind of solidarity that comes from being in the same boat.

Shared work around the house tends to make people more emotionally dependent on one another. This change seems to happen most when it coincides with a move away from the same-sex support group. Elizabeth Bott (1957) wrote about families that moved from long-settled inner-London neighborhoods to the suburbs, where mothers and sisters were no longer in the next street or the next house or the same tenement building, but a bus ride or a train ride away, at a distance where "dropping in for a cup of tea" was not practical. Those circumstances encouraged work-sharing around the house and a more companionable relationship between the spouses. Along with work-sharing went problem-sharing. On the other hand, work-sharing also encourages (as do the two wage packets) accounting of contribution to the household, and thus can be a source of discord. In short, the change that takes women to work outside the house also lets a draft of rationality blow over the nonrational foundations of family conventions.

What does this say about disengagement? Where the changes that I have just described are well under way, we are no longer in the land of the housewife and her nest egg saved out of the housekeeping money, no longer in the land of the peasant hiding in the woods or poaching deer, no longer with Svejk and his veiled mockery, and no longer in the presence of ceremonialized and licensed disrespect for authority that is a feature of carnival or soldiers' songs and chants. Nothing of that nature, nothing covert, is going on in the two-headed household. There is instead a debate and sometimes a fight that certainly is about whose writ will run where, about rights and duties. It is a fight between relative equals; not only are men and women more equally weighted, but so also are the values of rational individualism and of holism; the family no longer has the intrinsically superior value that once it had. That value has not vanished; it now shares the horizon with individualism, requiring in us, as MacNeice says, the capacity to split the vision and to make quick turns, to and fro, between one and the other. A split vision is also needed to make sense of the larger world outside the family.

AN EXPERIENCE OF HOLISM

Looking back at the philosophies of the various organizations fragmentarily portrayed in this book, the school, the army, the various universities, and thinking of the larger moral ambience in which they existed, I find nothing stands out so clearly in my recollection as the contrast between the holism predominant in the 1939–45 war and the individualism that prevailed most of the time before the war and quite soon recovered itself in the collective disillusion of the postwar years.

Sixth-form schooldays, in the early years of the war, provided a practical lesson in holism, in ungrudged and eager public service. The school had long had an Officer Training Corps and those of us who belonged to it, who had earned a certificate of competence (known as "Cert A"), and who had reached the age of sixteen, were enrolled (after Dunkirk) in the Local Defence Volunteers (later the Home Guard) and spent two nights a week, uniformed, armed with a rifle and two rounds of ammunition, on sentry duty guarding open spaces (like parks and sports fields) against invasion by German paratroopers.[9] Other nights we were Fire Watchers, protecting that

[9] Our uniforms were still more or less in the pattern of the 1914–18 war: puttees, breeches, and a tunic with brass buttons and a high collar.

ugly schoolbuilding from incendiary bombs, our weapons being a bucket of sand and a bucket of water and a stirrup pump. Most of the boys by then had seen violent destruction and some had seen death. The school was evacuated to the countryside when the war began, but returned to the city just in time to experience the devastating night bombing raids that were intended to halt industry and destroy morale. At such times, and because we were young, it would have been difficult not to feel the stirring of holism; one was part of the team.

I do not recall that team spirit as being in the mode of enlightened self-interest, the calculation that the one hope of *personal* salvation was being in the "body." On the contrary, I remember it as genuine holism, the motivation being nothing but duty. Nor was duty a stern thing that one must (perhaps reluctantly) do; it was more an intrinsic joy of involvement, a matter of emotion rather than of calculation. Such feelings are not entirely generated within the self; there was an endless ham-fisted jingoistic propaganda being thumped out. But again I do not in my recollection associate jingoism and those bouncingly overconfident newsreel and radio voices with the spirit of service. Nor do I think that there was any simple *direct* connection between external perils and a sense of duty, of service given on the principle of closing ranks against an enemy. The dominant intervening variable is the drastic social reorganization that was brought about in Britain by those external perils.

The ambient social structure was radically changed by the war. Most men of the right age and fitness were conscripted into the armed forces. Other men, and women, were directed into "war work," which for women could include service in the armed forces and their auxiliaries, in nursing, or in agriculture, but for most was factory work. The economy was centrally directed. Rationing systems were introduced. Consumer goods of all kinds were in short supply, and negative concepts from the experience of the 1914–18 war—"profiteering" and "black market"—were taken out and dusted off and put to use. I think it was experience of this new social ambience, the hard encounter with nonmarket distribution and manpower redeployment, rather than any "dignity-producing" propagandist jingoist onslaught, that nourished and developed the spirit of holism. In other words, adjust the circumstances and, other things being equal, people will of their own accord come to accept the ideas.[10] Create a *de facto* holism (as in the central direction and management of peoples' lives), and the spirit of holism will come to prevail. (It will not, as we will see, prevail in perpetuity, because the enforcement of compliance and even the creation of consent, bring with them experiences that are their own undoing.)[11]

There were other manifestations of the new spirit at this time, which at first sight are difficult to link with the new social environment. I am thinking of what happened to tastes in the performing arts and literature. Classics in literature, philosophy, and history had been available in cheap hardback editions for some time (for example the "Everyman" series). Paperback Penguins, which cost sixpence, had begun to appear in the late thirties. They covered a range that included not only thrillers, like those of Edgar Wallace or Agatha Christie, but also a large inventory of highbrow books, Bernard Shaw, Aldous Huxley, Shakespeare's plays, translations of Plato, histories, and so forth. Wartime hugely increased the clientele for such reading. There was a corresponding exaltation in musical tastes, the tone of which is sufficiently illustrated by the fact that concerts held to raise morale in factories could include piano recitals and chamber music. People stood in line to hear lunchtime piano recitals given throughout the war in the National Gallery by Dame Myra Hess. Between 1942 and 1944

[10]Experience is inseparable from ideas. *Ideas* (about how to win a war) caused the rulers to make the changes that provided the experience that encouraged holism.

[11]This, *mutatis mutandis*, is precisely what happens in the making of a soldier (Chapter 2) and in the soldier's disenchantment (Chapter 3).

the proportion of classical music played on records by the BBC went from 6 percent to 40 percent (Hewison 1977:155). Of course there were still "big bands" and crooners and music-hall comedians and paperback "trash." Loftier souls were pained by the middlebrow quality of what was put out (Beethoven's fifth and seventh symphonies and Tchaikovsky's piano concerto in B flat minor unendingly repeated), but chamber concerts and the classics and such cerebral programs on the BBC as the immensely popular "Brains Trust" had certainly not been so large a part of the people's taste before the war.

What caused the change? A cynical explanation would be that the market no longer called the tune, that individual preferences had gone by the board, and that workers got the music and the literature that the society's masters thought was good for them. In other words, taste, like goods and labor, was being centrally regulated, and perhaps the common people resented it but could do nothing about it. But that is not convincing; it would be hard to include the *sale* of serious books in that explanation. I also think that there were many who at that time acquired new tastes in entertainment and were grateful rather than resentful. Undoubtedly the new styles did emanate from an elite. But they were not imposed. They were adopted by others for the same reason that holism in general became the fashionable design: they were part of the package that constituted the new ambience, not a direct imposition by those in charge. The holistic person, in other words, is a serious "responsible" person, whose altruism encompasses "higher" tastes. In this philosophical package, frivolity, irreverence, degraded tastes, and general shallowness, all go along with individuality.[12]

There were other heavy and unfrivolous things in that pack-

[12]Cakes and ale are not a feature of holism, which is unsmilingly Puritan. The total absence of humor, even much of irony, from Louis Dumont's *apologia* for holism is a clear instance of this *gravitas*. Catch, for example, the tone of Dumont 1971.

age, the most salient of which was socialism. In the general election that took place after the defeat of Germany but before the capitulation of Japan, the Tories and their promise of capitalist free enterprise were firmly rejected, despite Churchill's rampantly charismatic standing. This outcome very clearly demonstrated the thesis I am arguing: that the compulsion to accept a new design comes less out of direct ideological manipulation than out of experience.

We, working-class boys in the sixth form in that school and in that industrial city, got our ideas about socialism more from Fabians like Bernard Shaw and H. G. Wells and G. D. H. Cole and from the Penguin Political Dictionary than directly from reading Marx or Lenin, still less from Labour politicians. With such mentors, socialism, in our eyes, stood primarily for justice and altruism and equality. For us that was the salient part of its *ideology*. The fact that it involved central direction of peoples' lives seemed a secondary matter (an attitude that indeed would please those holistic philosophers, Dumont for instance [1977:10], who maintain that hierarchy does not entail power).[13] But in fact everyone's salient experience was not of justice and the like, but of central direction. By 1945 people had, for nearly six years, lived inside a framework of practical holism that put the interest of the collectivity before that of the individual. The design for living had become internalized. Certainly people were tired of rationing and of regimentation and of the prevalence of bureaucracy. But they voted for the Labour Party, and against Churchill. They voted for the party that stood for and intended to continue and expand central management of the economy. In other words, by the end of the war holism had become the *habitual* ethic, what Dumont (1977:18–19) calls the "predominant trend," what people experienced as normal. "We have come to take war and its claims for granted—it is peace and the pursuit of happiness that now

[13]That argument is disputed in Bailey 1991a.

appear abnormal."[14] To experience something as normal is often, albeit by logical sleight of hand, to think it right.

Dumont's phrase is well chosen, if it is properly understood. A "predominant trend" is not necessarily one which is statistically the greater (always supposing it were possible to measure such things as individualism or holism). Rather it should be envisaged as the rule which is generally and publicly accepted as respectable, as the right thing to do, even if frequently not done. Thus, to engage in black market transactions was to earn disrespect, although at the same time it was believed that few people, given the chance, would resist the temptation to get something on the side. Men who lived by their wits and were adept at translating shortages into personal gain were called "spivs" and the folklore soon developed a category of gleeful tales about spivs who over-reached themselves and got burned in the deal. Even the aboveboard individualism, typified by Uncle George, who in prewar times could stand as a role model for the decent hardworking individual, was outmoded, no longer the predominant trend. Uncle George himself felt it his duty to serve the public good by undertaking voluntary war work (in the hospital boiler room), and later, although old and no admirer of the military, he joined the Home Guard.

BACKLASH

The habitual ethic that brought in socialism contained within itself the agency of its own reversal. First, even at the height of holistic enthusiasm there was a selective continuance of individualism, which in certain contexts people refused to see as being in conflict with holistic needs (although in terms of opportunity cost—time and energy—it certainly was). For ex-

[14]Raymond Mortimer, writing in the *New Statesman*, Sept. 30, 1944. See Hewison 1977:88.

ample, at school the singleminded individualistic drive to further one's own career by winning an Oxbridge scholarship continued undiminished, despite the distractions and the physical impediments of wartime living. I recall writing scholarship examinations in an unheated wintry college hall, wearing an overcoat and with an ordinary glove on the left hand and an open-fingered glove on the right. Moreover, although military service was important (and inevitable), one gladly accepted the nine-month deferment (with half-time military training) that made possible a first year in college.

Furthermore, the habitual holism that central direction nourished and that led to a sense of social responsibility and a conviction that collective human effort could not only win a war but also make a better society, the belief that altruism was the right and proper mode of interaction, could not conceal the fact that in practice society contained many individuals, who nominally might be "of the body" but all too often behaved as if they were not. They scrounged and they stole and they evaded their obligations, and their conduct showed clearly that, while the spirit of holism might be on their lips, it was not in their hearts. That kind of individualism might be shameful, but it was certainly not unthinkable. By the end of the war it had even become something to flaunt, casual disregard of military obligation being marked by the phrase "Couldn't care less!"

There was another kind of in-built saboteur, whose actions inflicted great and continuous damage on the spirit of holism. This was the person who conveyed, openly and harshly, the essential impersonality and unfeelingness that characterizes any bureaucracy. Uncle George ran up against the imperious matron. The grocers and butchers, who no longer felt the need to be polite to their customers, now bound to them by a ration book, became targets for abuse and for dark threats of what would happen to them after the war, when customers would again be free to shop where they liked. Officiousness became the mode, and the stock retort to any request was "Don't you know there's a war on?" That rude sentence is in fact the bare face of holism; it is a rebuke that one is putting oneself ahead of the general interest. Paradoxically, the matron and other officious individuals managed to work off their individual frustrations and find relief for themselves by abusing other individuals, who were in their power, for not being sufficiently "of the body." In that respect the entire society had become like the drill-square side of the army, intent upon stripping its citizens of their individuality, as the army stripped its recruits. For an individual thus reproached, the experience could only serve as an irritant that kept the spirit of individualism alive and made it grow.

In certain cases there was an in-built resistance to wartime holism, especially among those who saw themselves as having creative talent, particularly writers. In practice they seldom went beyond verbal resistance, and usually proclaimed their personal disengagement. Sometimes, as with D. H. Lawrence confronting the 1914–18 war, the idiom of resistance presents itself as the rawest individualism, a true-belief in the essential immorality of power, especially the power of the multitude.

> He would not enter into the army because his profoundest instinct was against it. Yet he had no conscientious objection to war. It was the whole spirit of the war, the vast mob-spirit, which he could never acquiesce in. The terrible, terrible war, made so fearful because in every country practically every man lost his head, and lost his own centrality, his own manly isolation in his own integrity, which alone keeps life real.[15]

Disengagement does not always have such vibrant militancy. Consider again military training. The process of total absorp-

---

[15]The passage comes from Lawrence 1960:216. The novel is evidently autobiographical. Lawrence in fact was physically unfit for military service and his fury was never put to the test of refusing to enter the army.

tion of the individual into the collectivity, as in the case of the soldier who learns to not-think and at the same time finds a complete identity for himself in the organization, may stop short at compliance, never reaching consent. John Burns had this to say (in *Penguin New Writing*, no. 19, January 1943): "All the time, working inside the mass of an army, all references and relations are to things also inside; nothing outside—countries, people, new qualities and new values—is noticeable except as the army comes to them, and you gradually stop looking at anything outside."[16] That is clearly not the voice of the mindless and sparkling enthusiast, earlier depicted as the product of military training and military dignity. Yet neither is it the robust voice of resistance; it is a form of resignation, preventing one's own total disintegration as an individual by giving compliance but withholding consent.

Much of the writing, especially the poetry, of those who volunteered or were conscripted into the services in the early years of the 1939–45 war resonates with, even when it does not directly describe, a struggle for individual integrity, an awareness that creativity was put at risk by regimentation. The moral issues were not straightforward. Unlike D. H. Lawrence in the earlier war, most writers felt the cause was just, and were moved by a sense of duty, by the compulsions of the holism that the times generated. Some also hungered for the full experience of war, no doubt seeing such experience as a fuel for creativity. But poets and writers in general have a vested interest in what they believe is their own uniqueness, that translates itself into a duty not to waste their creative talent. They are peculiarly resistant, as Svejk also was, to the moral takeover that regimentation demands.

The poet's detachment is essentially a self-infatuated detachment. It is difficult to turn this kind of narcissism into regimented not-thinking, because such people are thinking all the time about themselves and their own destinies and the contri-

[16]Quoted in Hewison 1977:85.

bution they will make, not to the collectivity, but to art; they are noncritically reflexive, egoistic, unused to doubting their own personal importance. Alternatively, they are reflective, given to meditation, which is the next best thing to cogitation for making an individual. This self-centeredness is one way out of the holistic prison, at least out of the bureaucratic version of holism. It is a withdrawal into the self, a kind of personalism that in some ways resembles a failure of nerve. (This is not the way of a svejk, nor of Uncle George. Both of them are rational and calculating and active in their own protection.)

The dialectical generation of opposition to a design for living is easily observed. It is particularly transparent, indeed explicit, in wartime creative writers, including those who, for medical reasons or reasons of conscience, were not in the armed forces. No one, in or out of the services, was exempted from the pressures that led to habitual holism; everyone suffered—or rejoiced in—the regimentation of wartime life.

> The thought of a future world bureaucratically organized, closely managed, authoritarian, technologically efficient and spiritually dead produced a response that was remarkably similar from all shades of the political spectrum. Whatever political complexion society would have, it was bound to be Philistine; the answer was to assert the rights of the individual.[17]

The individual was indeed "squandered in self-assertion." Here is Alex Comfort (quoted in Hewison 1977:177): "The State has consistently shown itself to be evil. . . . It has absolved us by rejecting individuality. . . . We now accept no responsibility to any group, only individuals." D. S. Savage (*The Personal Principle*, 1944, quoted in Hewison 1977:177) wrote: "Civilization's apotheosis, totalitarianism, which is ev-

---

[17]Hewison 1977:176–77. Communist writers, as one would expect, were an exception.

erywhere becoming an actuality, represents the final displacement of personal values within society. . . . Officialdom, which has always been the enemy of creativeness, is at last victorious."[18] And Stephen Spender:

> The creative writer, ignoring the depersonalized assumptions and generalizations of the State, expressing only his own relationship with the universe, expresses the experience of the whole humanity which consists not of a social mass but of a plurality of individuals each with his individual relationship with the external world. (Quoted in Hewison 1977:178)

Some writers (not Spender) withdrew into a genre that was called Apocalyptic or Neo-Romantic. "In the middle of a world war, when the individual was indeed mobilized, propagandized and directed by an all-powerful state machine, such arguments for 'personalism' had great appeal, and were taken up by magazines that came under Neo-Romantic influence" (Hewison 1977:115). The style was antirational, mystical, a magical denial of the present reality. Here is a description of the Apocalyptic writer by Henry Treece:

> His style will be prophetic, for he is observing things which less sensitive men have not yet come to notice; and as his words are prophetic, they will tend to be incantatory and so musical. At times, even, that music may take control, and lead the writer from recording his vision almost to creating another vision. So, momentarily, he will kiss the edge of God's robe. (Quoted in Hewison 1977:111)[19]

[18]An unusual and ironic association of "civilization" with "totalitarianism," but entirely consistent with the sentiment; civilization is citizenship, and citizenship is the tyranny, exercised through officialdom, of the Philistine majority.

[19]The apocalyptic vision, musical, prophetic, and incantatory, is with us still, rejecting still the constraints of order, and resonating still with a

THE RESPONSIVE PENDULUM

Backlash is found everywhere, not just among creative writers in wartime Britain. When a new style emerges from practice into rhetoric, and is made articulate and achieves influence, it is especially likely to generate (or re-generate) an opposing ideology. More exactly, enthusiastic proponents of an ideology provoke others, whose values and interests are being threatened by it, or who are just tired of hearing it, into opposition.[20] The dean's university, unintentionally but very quickly, brought into existence a party of Adullamites, who professed to be passionate about research and who set about covertly creating the substance of departments (without their form). In the opposite direction, eighteenth-century rationalism provoked a variety of reactions, not all consistent with one another, from the disenchanted. Some took refuge in romanticism, some interested themselves in the irrational behavior of individuals or of crowds, and others were driven into privileging the idea of a collectivity and endowing it with intrinsic value. That striking esthetic and intellectual elevation in wartime public taste—history, philosophy, chamber music, and the rest—was accompanied by the satirical buffoonery of a ra-

---

sense of effortless superiority. "Postmodern anthropology rejects the priority of perception, and with it the idea that concepts are derived from 'represented' sensory intuitions that make the intelligible the sensible 'resigned.' There is no movement from originary substance to derived 'spirit,' from thing to concept, nor from mind to material, nor from the real to the less real, for the mutuality of word, world, and mind, or of language, things, and selves is beyond time and space, located nowhere, but found everywhere, as in the harmonic reverberations of a chord never struck but always heard" (Tyler 1987:171).

[20]This is the *principle of Aristides*, so called to celebrate the Athenian who voted to ostracize Aristides, only because he was sick of hearing about "Aristides the Just."

dio show, "ITMA," which set a pattern for a long line of sub-
sequent similar entertainments ("The Goon Show," "Monty
Python," and the like) that mock the establishment and established forms and rationality and logic.

Any style of life is generated dialectically from its opposite.
But this process is more than a dialectic alone, a moving to and
fro, inevitably and automatically like a pendulum. These
movements and their underlying philosophies (the Enlightenment, romanticism, psychoanalysis, and the rest) are not entirely each others' creators. They also are a response to changing external conditions. Designs for living sooner or later are
likely to adapt themselves to changed circumstances; but they
do not do so instantly. The war and the structural reorganization of society in Britain gave habitual holism its day, but the
ending of the war did not at once undo centralism. There were
several more years of shortages and rationing, and, most significant, there was a government intent upon planning and central
control of the economy, doing some things that commanded
widespread support (for example, the National Health Service), and other things that aroused little interest except on the
part of those whose ox was being gored (shareholders in indus-
tries that were nationalized, including, as it happened, Uncle
George).

But the world had changed and was still changing, and in a
direction that severely dented the habitual holism of the war
years. In a sentence, the social structure that engendered wartime holism was more and more clearly seen to be ineffective in
peacetime. Disillusion set in. I do not mean that there was an
immediate hungering for free enterprise. How could there be,
when people remembered the decade of the thirties? I mean
that institutional life seemed once again to be out of control.
This perception was not primarily a matter of politics. Adven-
tures like the Suez war caused a mass protest, but political
actions in Malaya and Greece and Cyprus and even (more recently and more immediately) Ulster, while they aroused the

ire or the applause of purported leaders of public opinion, left most people fairly indifferent. Most of all was that true of the empire's dismemberment: the relatively civilized way in which it was done was a cause for relief and self-congratulation, except for a few like Churchill.

The disillusion arose out of domestic policies. There were some high points, including Mr. Macmillan's 1957 pronouncement, "Most of our people never had it so good." But most of the time things did not go well. For more than two decades the rampant sectarian holism of the trade unions caused economic chaos. Other nations—annoyingly, defeated nations such as Germany and Japan—had begun to prosper. Worst of all was the fact that no one seemed to be able to find a convincing way to deal with the situation.

The glass is falling hour by hour, the glass will fall for ever,
But if you break the bloody glass, you won't hold up the weather.

In short, there was a partial failure of nerve.[21] Collective efforts seemed pointless, because they led nowhere. There might have been rational solutions to the present distress, but nobody could say what they were, or could convince others to join in the effort. In such circumstances individuals sometimes turn inward, in the manner recommended by the Apocalyptic poets, not in search of a rational solution to their problems but to find personal salvation by withdrawing from the world. In fact in postwar Britain that did not much happen; we became less a nation of mystics than a nation of svejks, surviving on the back both of the government and of the unions. Eventually Mrs. Thatcher, by restructuring the economy and the society, purged the nation of its wartime habitual holism and made re-

---

[21]This condition is wonderfully described by Gilbert Murray (1951, chapter 4). The verse is from Louis MacNeice, "A Classical Education."

spectable again that form of individualism which is least un-
pleasantly represented by Uncle George.

External conditions constitute a world that exists beyond
ideas—"beyond" not in the sense that we may never know it,
but rather that it is not sufficiently comprehended to be under
our control. On the one hand we have ideas, which let us work
on the world; and on the other hand, there is experience,
which is what the world does to us. We experience the consequence of our ideas, of our designs for living, but we have
usually failed to anticipate accurately and fully—sometimes
not at all—what the consequences would be. Furthermore,
other events are taking place in the world that are not only
beyond our control but also beyond our vision. We may not
even realize what is happening to us, let alone perceive its
causes.

That we live in a world, both physical and social, that is to a
large extent beyond our control is a fact to be accepted; it can
rarely be antecedently changed. What we can do is adapt ourselves to circumstances. We can react after the event (assuming
we survive it) and change our ideas, our design for living, to
suit the new situation. We may even sometimes anticipate a
new situation and deal with it, by making the necessary
changes before it happens, thus, in a rather literal sense of the
word, preventing it.

Of course, as I have several times remarked, a "new situation" is something that we perceive and define, identifying it as
the cause of present or future discomfort and as the reason for
modifying our design for living. Those perceptions and definitions are themselves shaped by prejudgment, and consequently
are matters of argument. For the most part, when these arguments are about social matters, the "truth" is not identified
referentially, by testing it against some objective reality, but is
the prerogative of those in power. If everyone accepts that version of truth, they also accept holism and their social world is

absolute and orderly, without internal contradiction and without debate. It is also, however, unable to adjust itself to the changing demands of an external reality, for the holistic framework acts like a wall of mirrors, allowing people inside to see only themselves.

The world outside is mostly its own master, is seldom under the control of our prejudgments, and in the end must be allowed, as the price of our survival, to shape those prejudgments. Disengagement, it then follows, is like a window on reality set in the protective and necessary wall of collectivism. A world without some level of habitual holism—in other words, a world without society, a state of nature—is thinkable, but not realizable, even if it could be shown to be desirable. We are stuck, fortunately, with society, and the issue is not the presence of holism, but its pervasiveness. It is an issue because in practice no society, certainly no complex society, could exist without political inequalities between individuals: someone is always in charge. Then, if one imagines perfect holism, the only experience of an external reality that is allowed to influence collective decisions is the experience of those who dominate.

The remedy is individualism: the scientist who can extend his vision beyond the established scientific paradigms; the creative artist who exempts his art from established modes, even the selfish entrepreneur. Confirmation, gratifyingly, is to be found in the work of a master of holism, Louis Dumont, writing about renunciation in Indian religion. Certain renouncers of Brahmanical Hinduism, Buddhists and Jains, set a style (vegetarianism) which the Brahmans copied. That is, individuals extrinsic to the whole are able to modify it by their example. Thus we learn "something fundamental, namely that hierarchy in actual fact culminates in its contrary, the renouncer" (1970:194). In other words, the whole is made subordinate to the individual, and that is how collectivities stay in business.

Svejk belongs in the category of individuals, but he is different from the rest. In the end, all but him are vulnerable to the demands of holism: a "successful" vision, whether artistic or scientific or entrepreneurial or religious, is one that becomes established. Jains and Buddhists, starting out as renouncers, are in the end encompassed, gathered into a fold. But svejks are different. They are not vulnerable to the holistic virus; they live with it and are immune. They are the primitive and ultimate individuals, both living off and defying the organization; and defying it not only in their own material interest but also so that they may have the freedom to shape their own identities and bestow their services where they think best. Ironically svejks, who are innocent of political designs, truly exemplify, in a perfectly practical way, the Maoist ideal of "continuing revolution," but in a manner that does not bring the disaster that it brought on China.

There is nothing to be gained by single-minded advocacy of either individualism or of holism. There is not much to be gained by seeing a one-way Weberian drift toward impersonality and formal organizations, which are the hallmarks of holism. That tendency may indeed be discernible in our recent history, but movement in that direction, if unchecked, would be the end of us all. We learn more about ourselves and our lives if we look at the tension between individualism and holism and interpret it as a movement that swings to and fro like a pendulum. The situation is a contest, in which the individual is the opponent of the organization, or—teleologically—in which an organization, as the price of its own survival, must provide itself with its own enemies. The individual's problem is the desire to maximize both freedom and order, contradictories that get in each other's way. Formal organizations are caught in a similar bind; they want holism—unthinking consent—but, if they achieve it, cannot effectively adjust themselves to an ever-changing environment.

In that last phrase we have broken out of the hermeneutic circle, at least to the extent that understanding and interpretation of ideas include the notion that ideas are tools or weapons that affect and are affected by the experience of a world outside themselves. We see the world through our prejudices, hermeneutically encircled, but from time to time the world comes back to us in the form of experiences that upset those prejudices.

References

Adas, Michael
    1981   "From Avoidance to Confrontation: Peasant Protest in Precolonial and Colonial Southeast Asia." *Comparative Studies in Society and History* 23: 217–47.

Amis, Kingsley
    1954   *Lucky Jim*. London: Gollancz.

Azarya, Victor, and Naomi Chazan
    1987   "Disengagement from the State in Africa: Reflections on the Experiences of Ghana and Guinea." *Comparative Studies in Society and History* 29: 106–31.

Bagehot, Walter
    1966 [1867]   *The English Constitution*. Ithaca: Cornell University Press.

Bailey, F. G.
    1960   *Tribe, Caste, and Nation*. Manchester: Manchester University Press.
    1991a   "Religion and Religiosity: Ideas and Their Use." *Contributions to Indian Sociology* n.s. 25: 211–31.
    1991b   "Why Is Information Asymmetrical? Symbolic Behavior in Formal Organizations." *Rationality and Society* 3: 475–95.

Berger, Bennett M.
    1981   *The Survival of a Counterculture: Ideological Work and Everyday Life among Rural Communards*. Berkeley: University of California Press.

Berkley, George E.
    1971   *The Administrative Revolution: Notes on the Passing of Organization Man*. Englewood Cliffs, N.J.: Prentice Hall.

Bott, Elizabeth
    1957   *Family and Social Network*. London: Tavistock.

Brophy, John, and Eric Partridge
    1965   *The Long Trail: What the British Soldier Sang and Said in the Great War of 1914–18*. London: Andre Deutsch.

Burawoy, Michael
    1985   *The Politics of Production: Factory Regimes under Capitalism and Socialism*. London: Verso.

Burke, Kenneth
    1966   *Language as Symbolic Action*. Berkeley: University of California Press.

Burke, Peter
    1978   *Popular Culture in Early Modern Europe*. New York. Harper and Row.

Burns, Tom, ed.
    1969   *Industrial Man*. Harmondsworth: Penguin.

Clifford, James, and George E. Marcus, eds.
    1986   *Writing Culture: The Poetics and Politics of Ethnography*. Berkeley: University of California Press.

Coase, Ronald H.
    1937   "The Nature of the Firm." *Economica* 4: 386–405.

Constantine, K. C.
    1983   *The Man Who Liked Slow Tomatoes*. New York: Penguin.

Daiches, David, ed.
    1964   *The Idea of a New University*. London: Andre Deutsch.

Dumont, Louis
    1957   "For a Sociology of India." *Contributions to Indian Sociology* 1: 7–22.
    1960   "World Renunciation in Indian Religions." *Contributions to Indian Sociology* 4: 33–62.
    1970 [1966]   *Homo Hierarchicus*. London: Weidenfeld and Nicolson.
    1971   "On Putative Hierarchies and Some Allergies to It." *Contributions to Indian Sociology* n.s. 5: 58–81.
    1977   *From Mandeville to Marx*. Chicago: University of Chicago Press.

1980 "On Value." *Proceedings of the British Academy* 66: 207–41.

Gellner, Ernest
1989 *Plough, Sword, and Book.* Chicago. University of Chicago Press.

Giddens, Anthony
1979 *Central Problems in Social Theory: Action, Structure, and Contradiction in Social Analysis.* Berkeley: University of California Press.

Gilliland, Mary K.
1986 *The Maintenance of Family Values in a Yugoslav Town.* Ann Arbor, Mich.: University Microfilms International.

Gough, E. Kathleen
1956 "Brahmin Kinship in a Tamil Village." *American Anthropologist* 58: 826–53.

Gurvin, Larry
1984 *The Calvi Affair.* London: Pan.

Haraszti, Miklos
1977 [1975] A *Worker in a Worker's State: Piece-Rates in Hungary.* Trans. Michael Wright. Harmondsworth: Penguin.

Hardin, Russell
1982 *Collective Action.* Baltimore: Johns Hopkins University Press.

Hasek, Jaroslav
1973 *The Good Soldier Svejk.* Trans. Cecil Parrott. London: Heinemann.

Hewison, Robert
1977 *Under Siege: Literary Life in London 1939–1945.* New York: Oxford University Press.

Hill, Christopher
1988 [1970] *God's Englishman: Cromwell and the English Revolution.* London: Peregrine Books.

Hoare, Quintin, and Geoffrey Nowell Smith, eds. and trans.
1971 *Selections from the Prison Notebooks of Antonio Gramsci.* New York: International Publishers.

Hobbes, Thomas
1946 [1651] *Leviathan.* Oxford: Blackwell.

Hobsbawm, E. J.
1959 *Primitive Rebels.* Manchester: Manchester University Press.
1969 *Bandits.* London: Weidenfeld and Nicolson.

Hoggart, R.
  1958   *The Uses of Literacy*. Harmondsworth: Penguin.
Lancaster, Sir Osbert
  1938   *Pillar to Post: The Pocket Lamp of Architecture*. London: Murray.
Lasch, Christopher
  1984   *The Minimal Self: Psychic Survival in Troubled Times*. New York: Norton.
Lawrence, D. H.
  1960 [1923]   *Kangaroo*. New York: Viking Press.
Locke, John
  1946 [1690]   *The Second Treatise of Civil Government*. Oxford: Blackwell.
Lodge, David
  1962   *Ginger, You're Barmy*. London: Macgibbon & Kee.
Lukes, Steven
  1973   *Individualism*. Oxford: Blackwell.
Marx, Karl, and Frederick Engels
  1979 [1848]   *The Communist Manifesto*. New York: International Publishers.
Milano, Euclide
  1925   *Dalla Culla alla Bara*. Borgo S. Dalmazzo, Italy: Bertello.
Mines, Mattison
  1988   "Conceptualizing the Person: Hierarchical Society and Individual Autonomy in India." *American Anthropologist* 90: 568–79.
  1990   "Leadership and Individuality in South Asia: The Case of the South Indian Big-Man." *Journal of Asian Studies* 49: 761–86.
Moe, Terry M.
  1984   "The New Economics of Organization." *American Journal of Political Science* 28: 739–77.
Moore, Wilbert E.
  1963   *Social Change*. Englewood Cliffs, N.J.: Prentice-Hall.
Murray, Gilbert
  1951 [1912]   *Five Stages of Greek Religion*. New York: Doubleday.

North, Douglass C.
1989 "Institutions and Economic Growth." *World Development* 17: 1319–22.

Olson, Mancur
1965 *The Logic of Collective Action: Public Goods and the Theory of Groups.* Cambridge: Harvard University Press.

Phillips, D. C.
1976 *Holistic Thought in Social Science.* Stanford: Stanford University Press.

Redfield, Robert
1956 *Peasant Society and Culture.* Chicago: University of Chicago Press.

Riesman, David
1950 *The Lonely Crowd.* New Haven: Yale University Press.

Rousseau, Jean Jacques
1950 [1762] *The Social Contract.* Trans. G. D. H. Cole. London: Dent.

Roy, D.
1955 "Efficiency and 'the Fix': Informal Intergroup Relations in a Piece-Work Machine Shop." *American Journal of Sociology* 60: 255–66. (Also in Burns 1969: 359–79.)

Schwartz, Theodore
1975 "Cultural Totemism." In *Ethnic Identity in Cultural Continuity and Change*, ed. George De Vos and Lola Ross. Palo Alto, Calif.: Mayfield, 106–31.

Scott, James C.
1985 *Weapons of the Weak: Everyday Forms of Peasant Resistance.* New Haven: Yale University Press.
1987 "Resistance without Protest and without Organization: Peasant Opposition to the Islamic *Zakar* and the Christian Tithe." *Comparative Studies in Society and History* 29: 147–452.

Simon, Herbert A.
1947 *Administrative Behavior.* New York: Macmillan.

Smith, Robert J., and Ella Lury Wiswell
1982 *The Women of Suye Mura.* Chicago: University of Chicago Press.

Spiro, Melford E.
1963 [1956] *Kibbutz: Venture in Utopia.* New York: Schocken.

1980 [1979]   *Gender and Culture: Kibbutz Women Revisited.* New York: Schocken.

Tuchman, Barbara W.
1979   *A Distant Mirror.* New York: Ballantine.

Tyler, Stephen A.
1987   *The Unspeakable: Discourse, Dialogue, and Rhetoric in the Postmodern World.* Madison: University of Wisconsin Press.

Wade, Robert
1988   *Village Republics: Economic Conditions for Collective Action in South India.* Cambridge: Cambridge University Press.

Whyte, William H., Jr.
1957 [1956]   *The Organization Man.* Garden City, N.Y.: Anchor Books.

Willis, Paul
1981 [1977]   *Learning to Labour: How Working-Class Kids Get Working-Class Jobs.* New York: Columbia University Press.

Yallop, David
1985   *In God's Name.* London: Corgi.

Index

Library of Congress Cataloging-in-Publication Data

Bailey, F. G. (Frederick George)
    The kingdom of individuals : an essay on self-respect and social
obligation / F.G. Bailey.
        p. cm.
    Includes bibliographical references and index.
    ISBN 0-8014-2811-4 (alk. paper). — ISBN 0-8014-8078-7 (pbk. :
alk. paper)
    1. Self-respect. 2. Responsibility. 3. Social sciences—
Philosophy. I. Title.
BJ1533.S3B35 1993
302.5—dc20   92-29723